A Stranger to Myself

Farrar, Straus and Giroux

NEW YORK

A Stranger
to Myself

THE INHUMANITY OF WAR:
RUSSIA, 1941–1944

WILLY PETER REESE

Translated from the German by Michael Hofmann

Edited by Stefan Schmitz

Foreword by Max Hastings

FARRAR, STRAUS AND GIROUX
19 Union Square West, New York 10003

Distributed in Canada by Douglas & McIntyre Ltd.
Printed in the United States of America
Originally published in 2003 by Claassen Verlag, Germany, as *Mir selber seltsam fremd: Die Unmenschlichkeit des Krieges, Russland 1941–44*
Published in the United States by Farrar, Straus and Giroux
First American edition, 2005

Photographs used by kind permission of Hannelore Kern.

Map: GeoKarta, Heiner Newe, Altensteig and MHME © Digital Wisdom.
Map labels updated by Jeffrey L. Ward.

Library of Congress Cataloging-in-Publication Data
Reese, Willy Peter.
    [Mir selber seltsam fremd. English]
    A stranger to myself : the inhumanity of war : Russia, 1941–1944 / Willy
Peter Reese ; translated from the German by Michael Hofmann. —
1st American ed.
        p.   cm.
    ISBN-13: 978-0-374-13978-0
    ISBN-10: 0-374-13978-4 (alk. paper)
    1. Reese, Willy Peter.   2. World War, 1939–1945—Campaigns—
Eastern Front.   3. World War, 1939–1945—Personal narratives,
German.   4. Soldiers—Germany—Biography.   I. Title.

D764.R41713 2005
940.54'217'092—dc22
[B]

                                                            2005047893

Designed by Gretchen Achilles

www.fsgbooks.com

1   3   5   7   9   10   8   6   4   2

Foreword

For at least a generation after the conflict ended, the Western Allies sustained a historical image of the struggle against the Nazis in World War II that began with blitzkrieg and the Battle of Britain in 1940, then traced the campaigns in North Africa and Italy, followed by D-day in 1944 and the drive of Eisenhower's armies toward triumph on the Elbe. But little was known and less understood about the vast, misty struggle in the East between 1941 and 1945.

Today we have achieved a better perspective. We can see that the contest between the rival tyrannies of Hitler and Stalin was the decisive clash of the war, to which all else was subordinate. The United States made a critical contribution to the Soviet war effort, supplying aluminum, trucks, canned meat, radios, boots, and much else, without which the Red Army's advance to Berlin would have been difficult, if not impossible. It was the Soviets, however, who paid the overwhelming blood price necessary to defeat the Nazis, suffering the loss of some 27 million citizens against 1 million dead in the United States, Britain, and France combined. American and British ground forces killed some

200,000 Germans in North Africa, Italy, and Northwest Europe. The Soviets killed approaching 4 million.

There was never a low-cost shortcut to defeat a power as highly motivated, industrially mighty, and militarily proficient as Hitler's Germany. A long campaign of attrition was indispensable. It was fortunate for the peoples of the United States and Britain that this took place in the East. Implicitly recognizing Russia as the epicenter of bloodletting, the U.S. Chiefs of Staff made the decision to create only a relatively small U.S. ground army. General George Marshall wrote to Secretary of War Henry Stimson in May 1944: "We . . . have staked our success on our air superiority, on Soviet numerical preponderance, and on the high quality of our ground combat units." Marshall might have added: "and on the willingness of the Soviets to accept the overwhelming burden of ground casualties."

A degree of sacrifice was demanded from the soldiers of the two tyrannies that never could have been made by those of the democracies. If Britain had been invaded by the Germans in 1940 or 1941, it is impossible to imagine, however bravely defending soldiers might have fought, that British civilians would have eaten one another rather than surrender. Yet that is what the defenders of Leningrad did from 1941 to 1942. Marshal Georgi Zhukov was probably the greatest commander of the war, yet his feats of arms were achieved by the exercise of a ruthlessness unthinkable in Dwight Eisenhower's armies. When Zhukov led the defense of Leningrad, he stationed tanks behind his own front not to kill Germans but to shoot down any of his own men who sought to flee. The Red Army shot 167,000 of its own men for alleged desertion or cowardice in 1941–42 alone.

The most important "if" of World War II is to consider how long it might have taken to break Hitler's dominion of Europe, if he had not chosen to invade the Soviet Union. From the outset, the creation of an Eastern empire, the pursuit of *lebensraum* for the German people in the vast expanses of Russia, was central to the Nazi program. Hitler told his generals that a single campaign would suffice to crush the rotten edifice of bolshevism. He was extraordinarily ignorant of the industrial power of the Soviet Union, and rejected evidence of its potential. When the Wehrmacht suggested early in 1941 that Russia was already building more tanks and aircraft than Germany, Hitler swept aside the claim, though in truth Axis intelligence estimates of Russian production were too low.

Any notion that Germany's generals were not complicit in Nazi atrocities can be dismissed after an examination of staff studies made before Operation Barbarossa was launched. German plans required the systematic starvation of millions of Soviet subjects, to remove their grain and foodstuffs westward to feed the German people. There is no evidence that Hitler's senior commanders raised any objection to this diabolical vision. The purpose of Germany's war in the East was to enslave the Soviet peoples, no more and no less.

Yet even the Führer suffered moments of apprehension about war with Russia. When Goering sought to flatter him before Barbarossa, asserting that his greatest triumph was at hand, Hitler sharply rebuked his marshal: "It will be our toughest struggle yet—by far the toughest. Why? Because for the first time we shall be fighting an *ideological* enemy, and an ideological enemy of fanatical persistence at that." And one day at the Wolf's Lair, Hitler's headquarters in East Prussia built expressly for the invasion, he voiced unease to one of his secretaries about what lay ahead: "We know absolutely nothing about Russia. It might be one big soap bubble, but it might just as well turn out to be very different." The German army, which attacked at three a.m. on the morning of June 22, 1941, possessed 140 divisions, of which 17 were armored and 13 mechanized, with 7,100 guns, 3,300 tanks, 2,770 aircraft—and 625,000 horses. In a rare invocation of any higher power than himself, Hitler concluded a message to his three-million-strong host: "May the Lord God help us all in this struggle!"

Within a week, the armies of Leeb, Bock, and von Rundstedt were deep inside Russia, sweeping aside the ruined divisions of Stalin, taking prisoners in the hundreds of thousands. Guderian's armored spearheads had advanced 270 miles. Staff at the Wolf's Lair asked the Führer why he had not troubled to provide even a pretext for his assault, far less a declaration of war. "Nobody is ever asked about his motives at the bar of history," Hitler answered contemptuously. "Why did Alexander invade India? Why did the Romans fight their Punic wars, or Frederick the Great his second Silesian campaign? In history it is success alone that counts."

Some officers on Hitler's staff suffered their first spasms of doubt about the rationality of their leader during those weeks of triumph in Russia. Perceiving victory, Hitler instructed his planners to prepare a blueprint for an onward march to British India. Thoughtful senior subordinates began to understand that their nation was led by a man who possessed no ultimate vision of a peaceful universe. His only policy was unremitting struggle, until there were no enemies left to resist his hegemony.

Private Willy Reese, the author of this memoir, joined the German army in Russia that autumn of 1941, just as the heady sensations of success were being replaced by stirrings of fear. The enemy's resistance was stiffening. An awareness of the illimitable scale of Russia was seeping through the ranks. The first frosts of fall were harbingers of the deadliest foe of all—winter. Hitler had made no provisions for a long campaign, least of all to supply arctic clothing to his soldiers. When cold such as men had never known began to grip their bodies, to seize up their weapons and vehicle engines, in desperation they were driven to line their clothing with newspapers, for they had nothing else. Shortages of fuel, ammunition, spare parts, aircraft, and bombs started to assail the German armies, in the absence of planning for long-term war production.

Meanwhile, on the other side, the men and women of Mother Russia were accomplishing miracles of endurance and sacrifice to sustain their own struggle. Whole factories were shipped by train beyond the Urals, machinery reassembled in the icy wastes of Siberia, where workers labored, sometimes without benefit of roofs, to build tanks and planes to resist the "fascist hordes." Those who weakened were shot or dispatched to the camps of the Gulag, where they died of cold and hunger in the hundreds of thousands. Raw recruits were driven into action unarmed, with orders to pick up the rifles of the dead. Stalin's commissars vied with Hitler's soldiers in mercilessness. When Russians retreated, they burned the villages of their own people, to leave no shelter for the invader. When Russians were captured by the Germans, many were killed out of hand, while others were conscripted as porters and auxiliaries for Hitler's legions.

The Germans made a grave error in inflicting barbarism indiscriminately upon those who welcomed them, just as they did upon those who resisted. Many Ukrainians and other Russian subject peoples detested Stalin and Moscow's tyranny and were perfectly willing to assist the cause of Germany. Yet when they too found themselves victims of wholesale brutality, there seemed no choice save to resist. Through the years that followed, partisan war behind the front imposed mounting pressure on German supply lines. Attempts to suppress this by mass murder, hostage-taking, and devastation of civilian communities foundered on the Soviet peoples' extraordinary capacity for suffering.

War made Hitler a fantasist and Stalin a realist. In the first campaigns of 1941 and early 1942, Russia's dictator sought to direct strategy himself, and even to micromanage battles. He was personally responsible for many disasters. Yet by 1942, he had learned the lesson. Without sacrificing a jot of power over the Soviet people, he began to delegate military authority to able commanders—Zhukov, Konev, Rokossovsky, and their brethren—and to be rewarded with victories. These Soviet marshals were terrible men working for a terrible master. Militarily, they were gifted brutes. Yet perhaps only such people could have stemmed the Nazi tide and begun to roll it back. Stalingrad in the winter of 1942 was the turning point of World War II, while Kursk in July 1943 represented the last major effort by Hitler's armies to reverse the tide of defeat, with 2,400 tanks and 700,000 men thrown into a titanic encounter with 1.3 million men and 3,400 tanks of the Red Army, which the Germans lost.

For the men who fought on the Eastern Front, which often extended to 3,000 miles and more, their worst reality was that there was no escape save death. Germans and Russians alike, committed to action in June 1941, were expected to soldier on through the shocking heat and dust and mosquitoes of high summer, into the piercing colds of winter and beyond, with wounds offering a man's only chance of respite. German soldiers like Willy Reese were granted occasional leaves, but Russian soldiers could hope to see their homes again only when they had first seen Berlin.

On the Western Front, German and Allied soldiers would sometimes take pity on one another, not least by allowing medical staff to minister to the wounded on the battlefield. But in the East, mercy was unknown. An SS panzer unit woke one morning to find one of its own officers lashed to a haystack in the midst of the Russian positions. He had been taken prisoner dur-

matched. Never again, please God, will 6 million and more human beings find themselves locked in bloody embrace for four years, amid such extremes of climate as prevailed in Russia. The men who came home from the East were scarred for life by what they had seen and done, as was Willy Reese. Soviet veterans, eking out pitiful pensions, are today deeply alienated from their own society. They feel that what they suffered for their country is unappreciated. Indeed, the new Russia seeks to banish the memory of the Stalin era. Red Army men have a bitter saying: "It would have been so much better if the fascists had won—now we might be living like the Germans."

When Willy Peter Reese returned from the front, he wrote about his experiences with the heated enthusiasm of an aspiring author. He was sent back only to die at the age of twenty-three. Elderly Wehrmacht soldiers, in their turn, must pass their declining years in the knowledge that they served the cause of the world's most terrible tyranny, in a struggle that ended in defeat. This helps to explain why far fewer soldiers' memoirs have been published in Germany than in the United States and Britain, and why those that exist are important historical documents. They record an experience far beyond anything our own democratic societies have known. We should value their lessons accordingly. They stand as testimony to the extraordinarily privileged universe we inhabit today.

MAX HASTINGS
Hungerford, England
January 2005

Preface

We are war. Because we are soldiers.
I have burned all the cities,
Strangled all the women,
Brained all the children,
Plundered all the land.
I have shot a million enemies,
Laid waste the fields, destroyed the churches,
Ravaged the souls of the inhabitants,
Spilled the blood and tears of all the mothers.

I did it, all me.—I did
Nothing. But I was a soldier.

At the time Willy Peter Reese wrote this poem in 1943, he had been serving on the Eastern Front for two years. Pencils and paper, which were sent to him at the front by his mother, were his weapons against the craziness of this murderous campaign. He wore the uniform of a rank and file soldier in the Wehrmacht. He had four medals and orders across his chest, among them an Iron Cross, II Class. He didn't mutiny or run away. But he wanted to be a witness.

Now euphoric, now depressed, always tormented by lice and with an advanced craving for alcohol, Reese sets about turning his notes and memories into a single coherent text. In tiny handwriting, using every square centimeter of the page, he writes whenever he can, often by the light of his cigarette, as he crouches behind his gun. Repeatedly, he gets into arguments with the other soldiers about the single lamp. On the run from the Red Army, though sick with hunger, he saves his letter paper and leaves the butter behind. "That's superfluous, but writing I need to live." In his diary, which he later uses as a source for his manuscript, he notes: "The only thing that gives me a personal will to survive is my duty to express this war, and to complete my fragmentary works."

He did it. On home-leave at the beginning of 1944, he types up 140 pages on thin A-5 sheets. He is just twenty-three years old, and nothing like the young man who was drafted into the Wehrmacht at the beginning of 1941. The civilian Reese writes poems and plays, draws, composes music, delights in nature. He corresponds to the point of caricature with the image of the German "Dichter und Denker," the poet and thinker he feels himself to be and would like to become. Two years after being drafted, as the Wehrmacht is on the retreat from the Red Army, the sensitive youth, who was nicknamed "Pudding" by the young stalwarts at school, has become a dull veteran: "Who were we?" he asks. "Spiritually ravaged—nothing but a sum of our blood, guts, and bones." A Schongeist seeking comfort in the bottle, and mocking himself as a "genius on distalgesics." But he remains a scrupulous chronicler of his own decline. He writes down what millions of Wehrmacht soldiers have suppressed and remained silent about.

"I'm collapsing under so much guilt—and I'm drinking!" he complains in September 1943, as his unit, fleeing the Red Army, lays waste the land, blows up factories, enslaves the people, destroys the harvest, and massacres the animals. A little later, on a chaotic transport into the town of Gomel, he describes how the boozy *soldateska* of the master race make a Russian woman prisoner dance in front of them. They grease her breasts with boot polish. When a woman and her cow are shredded by a land mine, he confides to his diary that he and his comrades had "tended to see the funny side of the situation." By now, Reese, in some situations at least, much more closely resembles a different cliché than the thinker and poet: that of the German occupying soldier in the East.

His "Confession," as he subtitles his manuscript, leaves no room for the myth of a squeaky-clean Wehrmacht, misled and misused by a criminal Nazi clique. But it leaves plenty of room for sympathy with the fate of the mass of German soldiers who were on the side of the culprits, while themselves often being victims. Even in Hitler's war in the East, which was so manifestly criminal, there is not always black and white, not always a clear distinction between good and evil. The scale of the action is so vast that the single man—his pain, his guilt, his experience—is almost invisible.

Reese makes this war understandable, by precisely and soberly describing what happens to him. Even if he can only see a tiny portion of the whole, the character of the campaign shows itself—that and Reese's capacity to find words for the unsayable. As when he writes of some hanged Russians, who fell victim on some hunt for real or seeming partisans: "Their faces were swollen and bluish, contorted to grimaces. The flesh was coming away from the nails of their tied hands; yellow-brown ichor dribbled out of their eyes and crusted on their cheeks, on which the stubble had continued to grow. One soldier took their picture; another gave them a swing with his stick." Here is naked, unmediated horror.

What we hear is a writer who describes the principal experience of his generation—participation at the front during World War II—better than almost any other. The sixty-year-old manuscript is not merely an authentic document but a literary discovery.

With his individual experiences, the soldier Reese shows how war destroys the soldiers who wage it. The sufferings of winter marches are made present to us. He gives detailed descriptions of the effect of frost on feet. All at once it seems perfectly reasonable that a soldier, frustrated in his efforts to pull the boots off the body of a Red Army soldier who had frozen in the snow, ends up sawing through the dead man's lower thighs, and then standing the boots with the stumps in them next to the cooking pot by the fire. "By the time the potatoes were done, the legs were thawed out, and he pulled on the bloody felt boots."

As unsparingly as Reese writes about the chopped-off legs, so also about the amputation of sympathy. Humanity doesn't disappear overnight, and it never disappears completely. It is lost piece by piece. The "dehumanizing consequences" of war, which Ralph Giordano has written about, leave a trail through Reese's text that widens as the war goes on. As he describes his military training in the Eifel Mountains, his lamentations still have the sound of self-infatuated postpubescent warbling: "The plowshare hurt the fallow field of our souls." Soon it is replaced by the cold constatation of the ravage done to a man at war, without any metaphorical ornamentation.

It persists in the only seemingly absurd wish to get back from home-leave to Russia as soon as possible. "In a sudden fear of anything kind and beautiful, we found ourselves assailed by homesickness. We longed to be back in Russia, in the white winter hell, in pain, privation, danger. We didn't know what else to do with our lives. We were afraid to be home and now understood what the war had done to our souls." Not long after the fighting begins, he starts to feel "a stranger to myself."

Reese is no Nazi and, in spite of occasional prejudices, no racist either. He writes splendidly earthy hymns to the Aryan master race, saying, for instance, how "the round-cheeked plague of Browns / the West in its excrement drowns." But he is part of Hitler's invading army. He not only witnesses the sufferings of the Russian victims but participates in the feelings of the German soldiers. He doesn't seek to prettify his own role. On the contrary: He admits and examines all the feelings that cannot be squared with his sense of self, but that become more mighty as the war goes on.

Along with the state of emergency of body and spirit in the war, there is still euphoria, pride, the feeling of comradeship. And sometimes the understanding of doing wrong is eclipsed by the adrenaline rush of battle. Reese, to whom nothing is stranger than being a soldier, writes: "Men who otherwise were perfectly peaceable characters felt a secret yearning for horrid feats of endurance and arms. The ur-being in us became awake. Spirit and feeling were replaced by instinct, and a transcending vitality swept us away." Battered by waiting and uncertainty, the "committed pacifist" plunges into the fight. "I am proud of this dangerous life, and of what I have endured," he boasts to his friend Georg. Sometimes he even feels contempt for those who shy away from battle and danger—only to be revulsed by the change in himself. Between battles and bouts of drinking, he tries to rally himself, and insists that he believes in "what was irre-

ducibly human, some angelic force that was stronger than everything contrary, a sanctuary preserving whatever was best and
most characteristic in me across the gulf of the years." Reese offers not a balanced judgment from some moral high grounds,
but the report from a participant, hurting others in a murderous
war, and himself suffering. Much remains unfinished and am-
biguous. And with that he describes the condition of a man
robbed of all certainty.

For decades, no one was interested in Willy Peter Reese's
manuscript. But his memoirs might have helped make the day-
to-day reality of the common soldier during the war a part of the
general consciousness in Germany. This has not happened yet,
even with 18 million men serving in the Wehrmacht between
1935 and 1945. Jan Philipp Reemtsma, the patron of the contro-
versial exhibition on the Wehrmacht, "Crimes of the German
Wehrmacht: Dimensions of a War of Annihilation, 1941–1944,"
sees this as a consequence of a social arrangement that has long
governed treatment of the Wehrmacht: "There was a sort of un-
written contract: You be quiet about your heroic deeds, and we'll
be quiet about the crimes you perpetrated. In this way—with the
exception of what was said within families—there was silence
about personal memories."

The version of things in the minds of postwar Germans was
determined not by the accounts of millions of witnesses but by a
legend that began to be put about from the day after the war
ended in Europe. In the last Wehrmacht report, dated May 9,
1945, the German soldier received a sort of absolution. "Loyal to
his oath," he had "done unforgettable deeds in utmost devotion
to his people." Some senior officers were sentenced by the Allied
judges at the Nuremberg trials. But, unlike the SS and the
Gestapo, the senior command of the Wehrmacht was not con-

demned as a criminal organization. In the licensed German press in the years after 1945, there were many reports about crimes perpetrated by members of the Wehrmacht, but most of that generation pushed aside questions about their past. The priority was the rebuilding of Germany; there was only slight interest in shedding light on the past. What there was interest in was a type of comic and adventure writing that dealt with comradeliness, soldierly virtues, and standing the test of enemy fire—all of them subjects on which, from the point of view of the old warrior, no one else is qualified to speak. Nor did the bitter accusations of those children growing up in the '50s and '60s against their own fathers lead these to open themselves, and come out with the experiences that had marked their entire lives. Dealings with the Wehrmacht continued to be dominated by politics, thus blocking the view of historical truths and for a long time obstructing the creation of any social consensus about the past.

Today it is an obvious and largely uncontroversial fact that what the Wehrmacht conducted in the East was an unexampled war of devastation. Part of what is needed to understand Reese's text is an awareness of the environment from which it came. The data about the German rampage in the Soviet Union defy the imagination: some 27 million dead. More than 3 million prisoners of war lost their lives, more than half of those the Wehrmacht had in their power. In the territories of Eastern Europe that were under the control of the German armies, Nazi executioners did away with millions of Jews. It was the greatest abattoir in human history.

Reese responds to his situation as a soldier with powerlessness, fatalism, and submissiveness. Of course he is familiar with Clausewitz's famous dictum that war is an extension of politics by other means. Of course he senses that he is being used as a cog in a giant murderous machine. The war behind the front line hurts him the most, because it was directed against defenseless people. In a letter to his parents, he says he would feel better as conquered than as conqueror. But he joins in. His feelings and thoughts and witness, which he doesn't want to relinquish at any price, don't lead him to insubordination or resistance. In one sketch he draws himself on the way to Russia with giant boots and a grotesquely magnified rifle; farther down on the same piece of paper is another self-portrait, showing himself heading west with a book in his hand and a flower in his buttonhole. Some of the time, at least, the desire for a civilian life remains alive in him. But war to him is like a natural event, an irresistible, elemental force. For humanity, a world war was approximately what an earthquake was to a mountain range, he writes in a letter to his uncle. And so to him, as to so many others, despair at the political and military direction remains without consequence.

Shortly after the beginning of the war, in exile in London, the great publicist Sebastian Haffner estimated the percentage of the German population that was "illoyal" to the regime as high as an astonishing 35 percent, and rising. Haffner gives three reasons why this large number of frustrated and dissatisfied individuals was unable to mount any effective form of resistance: the extraordinarily powerful, unassailable position of the regime, the "non-revolutionary mentality" of the disloyal Germans, and finally "lamentable ideological confusion" and the dearth of new political solutions. All three arguments reflect Reese's position.

But they probably describe the thoughts of only a minority, albeit a sizable minority. The soldiers in the Wehrmacht comprised a straight cross section of the population. Among them were impassioned supporters of Hitler as much as resolute enemies. But all of them were desperate: It is evident that they urgently needed to find a justification for what they were doing. The Nazis' racist ideology provided one. Another possible way of making the barbarity tolerable was the recourse to a soldierly sense of duty, as was firmly rooted in the thinking of the war generation. "Help me, God," Reese, who otherwise was contemplative and self-sufficient, writes in his diary in hours of despair, "to say this *yes* and *Amen*, which I have so bitterly fought to achieve, and not to lose it, because out of negation comes the deep, dully burning pain." This seems to have been the way out for millions of people: a way of consoling themselves, of being able to stand it. From there, it is only a short step to the postwar silence that was meant to stave memory off.

When the war was over, nothing was heard of Reese for decades. Several thousand pages of letters and manuscripts were kept by his mother, as a shrine to her son's memory. In the course of the war, some things were lost, but most of it she was able to save. She preserved his writing until the time of her death—not even thinking of publication. Reese's cousin Hannelore, who had looked after the frail old woman in the 1970s, inherited, along with some old furniture, a box of manuscripts. Years later, she set about deciphering the pages, some of them handwritten and yellowing. In 2002—now well past seventy herself—Hannelore began looking for someone to archive Reese's writing, so that it wouldn't be lost when she died. She wrote to universities and publishers; few bothered to reply. Then, thanks to Stefanie Korte, a journalist on the staff of the German newsweekly *Stern*, for which I was working as a reporter, the vital connection was established that led to this book. One afternoon in December 2002, I spent several hours on Hannelore's sofa in Friedrichshafen on Lake Constance. There was cherry tart. The wonderful old lady showed me hundreds of poems, stories, and finally the war memoir. I sensed right away that I was onto something extraordinary. The following summer *Stern* published a long reportage on Reese's war experience. The book appeared shortly afterward and shot to the top of the bestseller list. It was followed by a book club edition and then a paperback. In a matter of months, sales had topped 100,000. "This book is a revelation," wrote the Cologne *Stadt-Anzeiger*, while the Hamburg weekly *Die Zeit* greeted Reese's memoir as "gripping reading."

Not until the '90s and a new generation began to ask after the truth did the daily experience of an ordinary soldier become an openly discussed theme. Numerous collections of field post letters are published. But anyone reading them will see a disturbing incapacity to talk about what is experienced. "Many common soldiers were rendered speechless by the grotesque reality of battle" is the conclusion of the Wehrmacht expert Wolfram Wette. What was needed was "the exemplary individualizing of a 'little man' in the uniform of a soldier."

Willy Reese is not your typical "little man." He is highly educated, a fanatical reader. He views himself as a poet and dreams of living in a free Germany. But his war experience is that of a normal draftee. And he was able to make a text out of it, in which this experience lives. He doesn't want to judge, he writes to his parents on Advent Day 1943, "but allow the facts and my experiences to speak for themselves." Much of what he writes in his manuscript is taken directly from his letters and diaries. He sets down what he experienced and what he felt. The literary form and ambition are unmistakable. Most of the details of his description are not possible to verify. It is possible that his report, written up from memory or with the help of sparse notes, may contain errors of fact. But it is beyond question that Reese wanted to show something absolutely genuine. He writes that war opens the "secret chambers of the soul." His manuscript enables us to penetrate them.

STEFAN SCHMITZ

A Stranger to Myself

The war began, and we saw God and his stars perish in the West. Death rampaged over the earth—he took off his mask, and his skull face grinned, chiseled with dementia and pain. We set out into no-man's-land, saw him dance in the distance, and heard the throb of his drums at night. And so he brought in his harvest of corn and tares.

He transformed us with his being. He showed us other names and dimensions, and his dreams marked the picture of our time. His shadow fell across our path. His thoughts filled the spirit of the seeker, and sadness, suffering, and fear sprang up from the seed he had sown.

Forced marches and dangers gave rise to adventure, but the conversation of the angels stopped at our graves. We, the nameless and the unknown, the solitary and the lover, the wise man and the fool, the rich and the poor, took up the fight with our destiny, and under the constellation of necessity, we found a role for ourselves in resurrection and carrion. We danced around his altar like will-o'-the wisps: the killer, the doomed man, and the victim. We yearned to know his secrets, the purpose of his riddles, and the meaning of his games with masks and disguises. We talked in our sleep like dreamers, and such things as hope, faith, and love acquired weight once more. From the hell of storms of steel, faith in destiny, astral solitude, and out of readiness to die, we plunged into the abyss of eternity, and at the bottom we found God's face among the wreckage and dust of our years.

In this way, death grew into our lives. In no-man's-land, he kept watch.

The war began, but my life didn't change. The great dying did not yet shake my world. I walked through the woods on the edge of the town and dreamed of foreign travel. I could smell sunshine in the leaves and sap; blue shadows hung under the ferns; noonday gold brushed the grass and mosses on my path. I loved beauty, the benediction and peace of the earth. The town sank in the smoke of twilight, the evening star was reflected in the river, and I walked home under a crescent moon and stars.

I was working in a bank. Cash, checks, and bills of exchange occupied my days, but my evenings were mine.

Little amours passed like an old game of sighs and desires, smiles and sadness. Often I sat up past midnight with my friends, discussing God and the soul, talking about poetry, music, and love. We played with words and pictures, but we were also serious and impassioned young seekers and inquirers. We lived as masks of the spirit, tumblers of God, fools of love, beggars of desire, gypsies of the soul, and strangers to our own time.

At night I would read while the wind sang outside the darkened windows, and the hum of the city broke against the peace of my room like surf, till dawn rose on magic gardens and dreams and on the lies and philosophies of books.

I went to the theater, and I went to concert halls to listen to the music of Bach, Beethoven, and Brahms. The defeat of

Poland meant less to me than a sonata or a poem. Most of my nights were given over to the fantastic tales and introspective legends I was writing at the time.

Then it was winter. Gardens and streets were snowed under, storms lashed the roofs, and the town sank in fog. The spirit went to sleep, like seeds, woods, and earth. I said goodbye to my adolescence. The paths of childhood, the peregrinations of youth, and all the roads of love led into the dark, and the hourglass shattered in my hand. I felt restless. Dreams, despair, and thoughts of death came to me. In my self-division, I started a cult of mirrors and suffered from my fate. I hastened through deserted streets on bright full-moon nights, read pernicious books out of sophistication and decadence, hid my face from God, and finally found myself at home in the void, a speck of dust in space.

Under my mask of intellectual exuberance, I lived like a ghost and sought refuge with whores and in wine. Fantasies of flight and deathly longings consumed me.

I met my Beatrice. Love taught me to identify beauty in decline; greatness and purity in ruins; dignity and hope in suffering; and blessing, transformation, and mercy in death. A new life began. Like a convalescent, I heard the March winds rushing, and I experienced the spring awakening of the earth. When I had to say goodbye to my love, I put my trust in God and the stars again.

The armies were waiting out by the west wall. I paid them no mind.

Like a storm wave, the war burst in upon the Netherlands, and I experienced the defeat of the Dutch like a vision. My thoughts revolved around art and humanism. There was eternity in what peoples and individuals had created. Every age and time made their contribution to the edifice, and whoever had fulfilled his duty could die easy. Names might lose their ring, those who had borne them might disappear as the grave digger mixed their corpses with earth and the wreckage of their works, but their spirits outlasted the ruins, their souls lived in the destruction and in the memory of future generations; there was no death. And so the war came to touch my sense of life. But when France laid down her arms, my life went on as though nothing had happened.

I went to the sea, to my favorite haunts on Darss. I walked the beach in storm and sunshine. I lay on the dunes and dreamed to the crash of the waves, listened to the crickets strumming of hot noons while Pan slept. I sang and whiled away the hours. A stray love flitted along like a butterfly. I strolled through the woods, collected mosses, pine needles, and leaves. Grasses and flowers were experiences for me. I looked for bison, listened to the singsong of the wind, and watched the sun go down over the sea. The sky blazed in apocalyptic colors; bronze and gold tumbled over the waves. I read on cool starry nights and hurried through rain and storm. Still intoxicated by the richness of the earth, drunk with summer and youth, I returned to the city . . .

Autumn gave me an induction in death and its various fruits. I loved it already, a sleep without dreams, the extinguishing of the candle, the sweet comfort of nonexistence after the effort, the seeking and strangeness of living. In the confusion of my days, I yearned for its quiet, but I was afraid as well of death, which never took the veil off its reality, whose peace was alarming, whose silence droned like a primal storm, and whose mills churned night and day.

It was winter again. I saw war and peace as mere intervals in the history of the world. I lost myself once more in endless nighttime conversations about the futility of life, the mask of God, the magic of the devil, and the tragedy of existence. I did my job by day and waited for the call-up to bring the turn in my destiny.

But in my thoughts and dreams, my hopes, aspirations, and desires, I was still living without reference to the war, and death was a stranger to me and only an occasional visitor.

I drifted like a shipwrecked sailor through the calms of fate. I was no longer a citizen of the world and not yet a soldier. On my twenty-first birthday I received my call-up for the beginning of February. I gave up my job, gathered together my manuscripts, locked away my diaries, and burned the fragments. Restless days without real activity dribbled between my fingers like sand. My bridges to the past broke; there was no path into the future. No star lit my way. Without hope, but not despairing either, tired and somehow feverish, I got through the emptiness of the waiting period.

One night began like a thousand others. But beneath its stars the change began. I dreamed of the threshold of a new life, and by morning I stood before my destiny as a different person.

My mother was asleep. The night wind cried outside, showers of rain danced across the roofs, and my reading light burned with its friendly glow. I sat over blank pages, pondered and asked, dreamed and sought, wrestled with gods, angels, and demons. And understood.

At first there was nothing but fear and foreboding. We stood at the gate to no-man's-land and felt the nearness of danger and pain. The years of darkness were beginning, as the stars had decreed. Like beggars, we left behind the wreckage of our youth, freedom, love, mind, pleasure, and work. We were required to subject our own lives to the will of the age, and our destiny began like a tale of duress, patience, and death. We could not escape the law, there was a breach in our unfinished sense of the world, and like a dream, the march into the other and the unknown began, and all our paths ended in night.

Nothing could be more antithetical to my nature than having

to become a soldier, to be anonymous among strangers, a toy at the whim of commands and moods, than having to learn the use of weapons with which I would fight one day for a view of the world that was repugnant to me, in a war I never wanted, and against people who were not my enemies. Like a condemned man, I hesitated on the steps to the scaffold and felt the sword graze my neck. The judge had broken the staff over me, and in my powerlessness I accepted his sentence.

That was my abdication.

I smoked; I wrote a line; I drained a glass of wine. The clock ticked; the light flickered along the spines of my books and on the piano. There were aromatic pine twigs in a vase, and Christ's thorn flowering. Hours dropped into the sea of time. The night advanced, and I kept my vigil, pondered, and dreamed.

The terror of the army years ahead left me no rest. I thought back on the last months of my own life. Like a hungry man facing a long period without food, I hastened through books, concerts, plays, and parties, hectic youthful amours, and thoughtful hours in the garden of youth. But that night, music brought me no consolation, comedy no forgetting of self, tragic drama no reconciliation with my own fate. Every instance of beauty served only to heighten the pain of farewell, and even wine sharpened the anguish of my thoughts. I leafed through records, memoirs, and accounts of the previous generation's world war, looking for a stance, a way to confront what could not be averted, to know what awaited me, and to understand the war, to learn my own part in it, and to force conflict, danger, and death into my sense of the world. But my reading was as unavailing as my conversations with myself and as every conversation with others, in the shade of melancholy and laughter.

I switched off the light, pulled on my coat, and quietly closed the door after me, so as not to wake anyone. The cool night wind riffled through my hair. The moon was hidden behind the clouds, no streetlight lit my way, and there was no one abroad. I wandered through streets and lanes like a stray dog. Everything I passed carried associations of longing and adventure, despair and mania. I went home and once more sat pondering in the ring of lamplight. Midnight came, and I was still up.

In the beginning was suffering. We put down the masks we had worn in the early light, draped the mirrors of our being and of our vanity, renounced happiness and the growth of the soul, and took on the features of anonymity. We had the feeling: It had to be this way. We had a lot of past history to atone for; now fate made us acquainted with the form of our repentance. We accepted it, like a monk the scourge. Under the mask of a soldier, we settled our debt, and to atone for past lives of deception, frivolity, and illusion, we consecrated ourselves to pain and danger. We were ready to suffer.

Travel was not in my thoughts, any more than adventure, sowing seeds, or a secret maturation.

The clock hands spun around. The hourglass scattered its sand. The distant roar of mines, mills, and ports beat against the window. Footfalls echoed away. The loving and the lost were all long since asleep. My room became an island in the cosmos; this was where the light burned for my solitary thinking, my questioning, and my guessing.

The future was determined by the years ahead, of soldiering. Our fate disentangles itself, and the form acquires definition in what is to come. We were looking for the future. We had a lot to offer and to desire, and now all streets led into life. Fate was something vague that had barely touched our friends, encounters, books, and dreams. As yet we were not marked by anything substantial, anything experienced and lived. But now pitiless life would shape us. We would ripen in denial, survive in hostility, and preserve what was ours in battle. War, the father of all things, was showing us the way. Questions and interpretations loomed in the distance, and we guessed at a good outcome. Our essence was ripening within us; nothing divine could be taken from us, so long as we kept faith with our humanity. The man would emerge from the wearer of masks, being from appearance, and so would stand before God.

I accepted the necessity of what lay ahead. I no longer saw my soldier's time as a cross to bear. I was all set to live.

My mother awoke. She saw there was a light on in my room, and she came in and silently stroked my hair. Then I was once more on my own. I brought more wine, filled my glass, drank, and sighed heavily.

I didn't want my years of destiny. All the powers and forces within me refused to allow the strange, the hostile, to enter. The future remained a hell, and my assent did nothing to diminish my fear or struggle. Only my suffering and hoping helped. Nothing beautiful, lofty, or pure happened in no-man's-land. God did not dwell on battlefields, and the spirit as much as the body died in the trenches. Death held sway in war. What was best in me would be destroyed, and only what was rejected would molder away. If I ever came home, then a different man, destroyed, marked for all time, someone transformed, would stand before the mirror. Then I would wear the brand of death and lead a ghostly existence with the dead in twilight and night.

I emptied my glass. My head ached; my hands shook; my heart beat irregularly. The night was still blue and windy, and I found peace.

Life would not permit of any no. Even the most terrible thing wanted to be sanctioned by an amen. I would have to learn to want destruction, to reject being in deed, as I had often done in word and thought, and in this way to give a grand affirmation to anything that might happen to me. I would have to become as the law decreed, to live or die as my star ordained. No refusal, no will, could change my destiny. Life would be lived whether I wanted or no. I just had to live it, to be it.

I ate a piece of bread and lit a candle. In its flame, I burned the pages I had covered that night; then I opened the window and scattered the ashes outside.

Dawn dimmed the stars. Day broke, and life went on. It came over me like an awakening. Dreams and images blew away. I looked to the light. Solitude was at an end. Numberless companions were on their way to me from all over the world. They were bearing torches, death's-heads, and banners, and their singing rushed into dawn and attack. Like a column of pilgrims, they were marching into the distance, and I, nameless, went with them.

We had lost our masks, but our essence remained with us. Abroad, in life and suffering, our forms ripened, and in the immortal soul, all travails even on the brink of death were turned to light. The spirit transformed things and appearances into new life. The plowshare hurt in the fallow field of our souls. It was no longer a matter of happiness, sadness, life, death. Only fate made sense, and a man's mission. We grew and matured as necessity made us. The mills of suffering ground at the brittle crystal, the fire of warfare purified outlook and process, and death led us within ourselves. But we kept the face of God above us like stars. We lived life, as it really was.

And so I went to my recruiting inspection, as into a ceremonial Advent.

I became a soldier.

The Soldier

The time of adventure began, but at first war was nothing but play. The summer sun seared the rocks and forests of the Eifel. Fields and pastures withered; the heathland crackled with dust and fire. Villages and hills flickered in the noonday heat, and dust from the troop exercise ground at Elsenborn was scattered over gardens and roads. Morning mists blew over alders and birch saplings by the roadside, there was a sultry steaminess in evergreen and broad-leaved trees, and at eventide the shadows fell far across the land. Often not a leaf or stalk stirred; only the crickets fiddled a little somnolent music. Then cool and silence blew soothingly abroad into the night.

I had been a soldier for some months and now wore the warrior's mask with assurance, irony, and patience. Never had substance and appearance been so far apart with me. Like a dream, obedience, commands, and the toughness of service hushed past me, leaving not a trace. I withstood the training like a sleepwalker. I walked in step and carried my rifle. Like a machine, I learned how to use a machine gun and a light antitank gun. An hour's worth of reflection was enough to bring out the sadness and despair, emptiness and fear, rage and pain of my days. I did not complain about being alone. I loved it, but sometimes I was overcome by feelings of helplessness and abandon. Something inside me wanted me to remain as I had been before my draft. Even that became difficult. All thoughts of the future fled as from a huge horror, and I was barely able to overcome the shocks of the soldier's life. But I got used to it, to never being alone, but always a stranger among strangers, separated from the others by spirit and soul, manner of life and beliefs. I went through the inevitable acclimatization, but I never allowed the noise and the monotony of the day-to-day into my private kingdom. Before long I had recovered the confidence and irony to get through it without taking damage.

I lived in the dark. Ghosts lurked everywhere. Fear, disappointment, and a continual grief marked my sorry path. It was better then to believe in the most fleeting dreams than to be helplessly at the mercy of doubt and uncertainty. I couldn't live without the tiniest shimmer of hope. Everything on earth was growth and transformation, and as the surface changed, so the essence of a man ripened within. My dreams showed me pictures of my hidden evolution, even if I, dazzled by the days, was unable to understand them when, for a few seconds at a time, they showed themselves. I was asleep, but it was precisely at such moments that the reality and nobility of life struck me most forcibly. In this way, for all my errings, I was able to find my way back to the man I had been before the outbreak of war. Everything was a sort of homecoming to me, even if I often failed to grasp the path and the destiny, and at times I was able to shape my own life as I pleased. I was made happy by the small joys of a soldier's life, a book, a glass of wine, some music, and a contemplative evening in the Eifel Mountains. Fate was often kinder to me than I expected and taught me to trust myself again.

Barracks life and drills seemed worse to me than war, just as the school of life took life more seriously than God and the world did themselves. Because now the metal that had been won from youth's ore was hammered to steel, and I had to serve as anvil. The platoon was made into a fighting unit, the individual to a cog in a machine, able to fight, to overcome hardship, to suffer privation, and to attack; willing to suffer and to die, prepared to obey and to do without for the sake of the war. And so the cannon fodder was brought up to snuff. The raw material was given its form, and I took the soldier's mask more seriously. I played my part in the great drama of assimilation, without any spectators on the stage of my destiny. The phoenix burned, and I gathered up its lost feathers. I had too much time to be able to think of myself. My existence took place within me, mostly unreflected in external events. But the change was in progress. I was becoming a soldier.

Mists like white smoke climbed out of the fields and meadows. I stood on sentry duty, feeling I was at the end of the world, in some foreign land, among foreign people. Evening came down out of a silver gate of clouds. The land subsided at my feet. Grass and shrub, near and far, slipped into shadow, haze, and scent, and silence covered the earth once more.

I set down my rifle and went looking for grasses and mosses. My boots grew wet with dew. I sniffed the fog and the chill of dusk, took off my steel helmet, and let my hair blow in the wind. It stroked my forehead, like tender hands. I was in love with every flower, every stone, and gave myself over to my looking and listening.

The past few months had sharpened my eye for the beauty of small, simple, familiar things. I saw the world more alertly. The dust and gray of the city dropped from me, and I experienced the improbable beauty and delight of the world more than I ever had in the fullness and exuberance of the summers in Darss. A flower by the roadside was a kindness to me, a forest under the scorching sun, a spider's web pearly with dew, a butterfly, and the dance of midges at eventide, the plashing of a brook, and a lizard sunning itself on a hot stone. All these were experiences to me. The growth of wheat, bindweed, and poppy taught me to stand there with as much patience as theirs, and their innocence moved the masked man and soldier just as a repentant sinner might be moved by the comforting hand of an angel. But I was also painfully and burningly aware of the gulf that separated the dove, the shrub, and the tree from the war; and the soldier from all the love and blessings of the earth. I was no longer jaded and indifferent but found myself, like an insect with superfine antennae, shaken by the goodness and peaceableness of the earth. That was the only reason I was so grateful for the frost of early blue mornings, for daybreak and dawn chorus. It was as though, in my sorrow and cruelty, I had to be reminded of the divine. No evening seemed so mild to me as the dusk after a hot, exhausting day of misery and soldierly torment. I felt the star-bright nights, the rapture of moonlight, violent storms, and tireless pattering rain more intensely than anything I had done by the sea.

Also, the simplest facts of human life—sleep, a piece of bread, a sup of well water, a kindly word—all these, after long disregard, became precious to me once more, and anything beyond the minimum I took as an unmerited kindness.

But that night I was taken by a violent yearning for my past. My sheltered youth pursued me with gorgeous scenes. There were many things I had not done, and the future sat in front of me like a raw block of marble. I could suddenly hear Moorish dances; I saw the stage, the dancers, I heard the Gypsy song and the keening voices of the girls, the magic and drunkenness of Dionysiac music, and I wept for my homeland and my personal fate. I left nothing out, and as I drank the bitter cup, I saw the purpose and the significance of time. Scenes, music, and stars wandered into my dreams . . .

On the Hohes Venn, the heathland was ablaze. The fire chewed the turf under the tindery ground and threatened woods and fields, as it kept flickering up in new places. Foresters and soldiers were set to fight and quell it, and in the evening we were sent out to serve as firemen.

Smoke obscured the slope. The smell of burning flowed down into the valley; dust and ashes came down on our faces and shoulders. As the evening cooled, we climbed up. Dusk fell early. Smoldering fires played like will-o'-the-wisps on the forest edge. On a height, little flames flickered up like rows of lanterns, lit by dwarfs and heath spirits in the wind.

We ate our bread, looked out a camping site for ourselves on the soft needles between the pines, put up a screen of branches to protect us from the wind, and rolled ourselves into our thin blankets. One man kept watch. Very slowly the humus gave back the warmth of the bygone day.

I lay there a long time with eyes open. Stars glimmered in the branches, spun incredibly slowly over the trees. Wind whispered in the boughs, dew fell, and the earth exhaled mist and moisture. So I found my home in the cosmos. I had grass and needles for a bed, the sky for a ceiling. No walls separated me from God and the weft of life. I lay as sheltered as in the heart of the world.

Some Walloon foresters came and sat by me. They talked about their work, their wives, about the work and the happiness of a conquered people that never understood the war and was happy simply to endure, now that it was over. At midnight they took their leave of me, as of an old friend, and left to protect their huts from the creeping subterranean fire. I was glad. I never saw other peoples as enemies; there was always a bridge from man to man in quick time. They sensed the peaceable man under my uniform. The only enemies I ever found were around me, and within me, in the self that was fighting against my destiny and imperiling me. So I thought, and fell asleep.

I woke shivering at dawn. The fire had gone out overnight. Fog and smoke mixed to a thick haze. We went back down to camp . . .

We traveled to Monschau, and I breathed in the air of my old city. Life wasn't so bad; it was just me making it unbearable for myself. As if, in my obstinate hatred for war and military, I insisted on suffering from them.

At noon we marched past the lake at Robertsville, over hills and narrow forest paths, into the valley. A stream flowed under beeches and alders, trout flashed over the stones, algae shimmied in the current, and feldspar and quartz glistered on the bottom. We climbed steep slopes to a ruin, and there in the ruined castle we set up camp among wild fruit trees and blossoming shrubbery.

As evening fell, we scaled the wide tower, lit a campfire, and sat on the crumbling masonry, amid ivy, brushwood, thorns, and wild vines. We emptied a small barrel of beer, smoked, and sang songs of soldiers' lives, love, going to war, and death, full of the melancholy-beautiful bliss of death that I once felt when listening to Haydn's Military Symphony. Flames flickered, stars danced, shadows covered us, the scent of wood, juniper, and mountain ash climbed up to us, the night wind burst on rock and bush, and the moon sailed through the dreamy night. The call of a screech owl resounded in our silence. We sat together as though resting from a long journey. In that hour I felt at ease in my company, one of many who shared the same destiny, the same garb. Though not necessarily of one mind, we were just adventurers abroad.

So I was a soldier for a few hours at least, even in my heart, and felt an early intimation of gratitude to life and fate, which taught me that many things could happen only in war and in the mask of a soldier. I felt the soldierly spirit that identifies beauty in the midst of sweat and pain and welcomes the hour of relief at the end of obedience and punishment. Secretly, though, what I loved was the feeling of returning to my self, which opened its gates. What I was responding to were romance, youth, and a whiff of a different freedom—never weapons, never war. My yearning always remained awake, and my homesickness unrolled its carpets over all things and experiences. I was still only at the beginning, and what was ahead lay in front of me as in a locked chest. Untrodden, the wide, wide world stretched in front of me.

I was still living in my own kingdom, thinking of the cosmos, the search for God, wild imaginings, dream and grotesquerie, which, even in self-division, spiritual anxiety, despair, and questioning, I preferred to the soldierly world of masks.

Night rain whooshed down on our tents, drumming on canvas and leaves. The following evening we marched back to Elsenborn . . .

The war games went on. We practiced with flags, blanks, and dummies, and our victory was never in doubt. We tossed our enemy aside. And the Wehrmacht reports carried nothing but victorious encirclements, advances, and extraordinary numbers of captives and booty from the Russian campaign, where our destiny was pushing us. We served the imperative of history as specks of dust in the whirlwind and were privileged to participate in the end of our world.

So the introduction to my adventures ended with intimations, dreams, and signals whose interpretation I left to some future date and later forgot.

We returned to barracks in Cologne lean and strong and sunburned. Our posting might arrive any day. I took what the city could offer me: amours, books, concerts, plays, variété, and thoughtful hours in the cathedral. I went home, saw my friend once more, and drank the night away with my comrades. Uncertainty and expectation were features of my days. I didn't worry and felt strangely impatient for what was to come.

One day I found my name on the list. I was kitted out and equipped, said my goodbyes at home, and set off on my great Russian adventure.

And so the war began for me as well.

Polish Intermezzo

At dawn we marched to the station, with pack, steel helmet, and rifle. It was raining, the weight pressed on our shoulders, and within us we felt the sadness of departure. The women on the streets had tears in their eyes; the girls smiled at us.

We were put on trains, and the great adventure began.

The train rumbled through the late summer, into the rising sun. It felt humid in our goods wagon. We sat on hard, shaking benches. On the floor was a thin covering of well-trodden straw. Our baggage was stacked in the corners; our blankets were full of dust and chaff. Rifles and belts struck the walls in the tempo of the rattling wagon, and the wheels sang the never-ending song of the rails. A hubbub of voices, song, card games, sleep, and laughter surrounded me, and I was afraid to reflect. And so I read, without knowing what I was reading or understanding it.

We hunkered down in the doorways and saw the villages, fields, woods, and pastures of home slip past us, waved to the girls, and sang our songs into the rushing wind.

It wasn't much before midnight that we finally fell asleep on the boards, shaken about in our carriage, pursued by dreams, and we woke not long after. It seemed to have barely gotten dark at all.

For a long time I looked at the flat meadowland with its half-timbered houses and scattered groups of trees. Sometimes the scenery reminded me of the Darss. Towns and empty expanses rolled by. We kept seeing birch trees beside the line, and yarrow, Aaron's rod, and grass bending in the wind as we passed. The same little wood seemed to come round again, the solitary tree, the field track, the road, the stream. The aspect of the landscape was slow to change.

I was indifferent to the noise and commotion of the soldiers in the wagon with me. I was quiet and calm, oddly equable. When I looked at the ordinary people outside, working in their fields and gardens, I remembered that I was traveling to Russia to fight, to destroy seed and harvest, to be a slave of the war, but then, out of danger and nearness of death, I would feel a lofty freedom and an almost pleasurable sense of life. I was overcome by homesickness. Sorrow at parting and loneliness made me sad, and of course I was frightened of what lay ahead. Certainly there was nothing familiar.

In spite of that, I wasn't wrestling with my fate. I yearned with a passionate impatience for whatever was awaiting me. I was still young enough to desire anything new, to relish the excitement of the journey, and to intoxicate myself with dreams and fantasies. I didn't think much of death and danger; distance pulled me toward it. The array of what I saw outside and the atmosphere of our departure filled me with an unspecified joy. Melancholy recollections mingled with stoicism toward the present; worry and grief with a boisterous pleasure in being alive. I felt as unhappy and consumed by bliss as if I were in love.

And so I entered the magical space of adventures. It was the beginning of a long journey.

The next night also passed without sleep. It was very early in the morning when we crossed the border into conquered and once more partitioned Poland. Flat country and distant hills characterized the sparse scenery. Stubble fields with shocks of corn, pastures with the drying hay from the last mowing of the year, small villages, and low, functional houses, wide streets, and neglected gardens filled in the space between the cities: Lódź, Kraków, Katowice . . . Barefoot women went about their work, with kerchiefs tied over their dark hair, and skirts bleached to some indistinguishable color by the sun. Ragged, neglected children begged for bread. They ran along beside the train, holding out their bony hands, or stood there accusingly, an image of hunger and abject poverty. Their pleas and their thanks sounded equally foreign to my ear. We had little enough to eat for ourselves. Their poverty was strange to us too; it didn't resemble our native poverty in Germany, and we didn't really understand it. We were not yet acquainted with hunger and inflation; it was our first meeting with a people who spoke a different language, with a different attitude, another purpose.

I saw no enemies, only conquered people. Only strangers. No path led to their souls and spirits, and from the moving train I had little sense of their day-to-day existences, their happiness and their grief. I did nothing and didn't reproach myself. I was just tired, pale, and I dropped off from time to time.

We stopped in Kraków. At midnight I was standing sentry on the rails. Over me sparkled innumerable pallid stars. A yellow moon appeared between loose clouds, turned a deep orange, and sank in a gory red. Barely a signal, barely a faraway light shone to me in the dark. I shivered, and my eyes were dropping shut.

We traveled onward.

In the morning we reached Jaroslaw, the new frontier town on the San. We piled out.

September sun lay on the platform of the little station. The Russian Empire began on the far side of the river . . . I sat down on a stack of boards, felt the warm sun in a tired way, and watched Russian POWs at work. Bearded faces, unkempt hair, empty eyes, and ripped uniforms all presented an image of sorry homelessness. Every movement that was performed was dull and slothful, and the guards swore and hit out with sticks and rifle butts. I felt no anger at the ill-treatment of these helpless men, and no sympathy either. I saw only their laziness and their obstinacy; I didn't know yet that they were hungry. I was glad we had stopped moving for the moment and that we had another interval of time. I was completely preoccupied with my own destiny . . .

We picked up our knapsacks and marched to the barracks. Ocher houses with lofty windows behind dusty trees were redolent of an atmosphere of soldiery, service, and ugliness. We moved into bleak little rooms, with cockroaches, dust, and hunger. There our shared privation and distance from home made us into comrades. Secretly, though, everyone remained isolated. There were no bridges from one man to the next.

We marched out every day. With knapsack, coat, and blanket roll, with storm pack, bread sack, and rifle. Singing, we marched through Jaroslaw and followed the tarred roads into the outlying woods and hills. With singing and humor we battled through our exhaustion. We had to practice marching because at the time that was the only task we expected to be given during this war. We marched in rain and shine, and thunderstorms broke over our heads. We draped canvas sheeting about us, the wet dripped off our helmets, and our rifles sprouted rust like fungus.

I didn't often go into town in the evenings. It wasn't that it was strange to me, the towns of this world aren't so very different, and at that time I didn't have much of an eye for fine distinctions. It was a wretched caricature of a small town in Germany, without any amenities except a little library and a tolerable schnapps in some of the bars. I didn't enjoy being a soldier among a conquered people. I felt strange and excluded; I felt ashamed of my presence there and often felt responsible for the people's misery, as when an unmerited hatred seemed to strike at me from all directions. I bought cake and fruit to supplement the sparse diet, sometimes played the piano or read in the soldiers' quarters, where we had a wildly varied selection at our disposal; then I would return home at night with my companions through the darkened town. We sat in smoky bars and drank the garish and syrupy schnapps. Later on we would stare at girls and women, but there were no encounters. I wasn't immune to the tender blond or Gypsyish charms of Polish women, but I was too ashamed to go after love in the midst of this foreign people, and the squalid brothels only disgusted me. Eros took other paths, in our jokes, and everyone who told stories became his own Don Juan or Casanova. Only self-restraint and collective living could master what lay ahead of us. And so we lived like monks.

Usually I was on my own in the barracks reading room, and I wrote my letters, aphorisms, and poems and tried my hand at eerie tales. From my fables and fantasies I increasingly withdrew to philosophy and problems. Often serious conversations would go on till deep in the night. We were looking for some principle or backbone to help us bear our fate.

Every day the tormenting emptiness within me deepened, like the grief of a homesick child, while at the same time I ate the bread of what was to come and painted frescoes of my future.

I was a soldier in the same way I had once worked in a bank. I accepted my lot like a job I disliked and so saved myself some mental strife. At first every adjustment was difficult. But my spirit remained true to itself, and what I experienced wasn't wasted. But what I gained, the future had to confirm. I came to my senses more and more, and left to my own devices like a shipwrecked man on an island, I became ever more thoughtful and introspective during my solitary hours.

Broad awake, I stalked through the days of incipient destiny and soul–making. When the autumn wind bent the yellowing trees, when red foliage flew and the storm blew over the hills, when rain clouds chased in front of the sun and the distance expanded under the changeable skies, I felt again that heightened feeling of intoxication that once had been engendered by my summers on Darss. Now my yearning for those free times of wandering and growth became part of what I felt, a yearning for a return to the familiar beauties of a world more my own. Every fine hour deepened me, homeless, all on my own in the foreign place; landscape, tree, and shrub all acquired deeper meaning and fresh purpose. My senses became acuter, I looked more consciously and tenaciously than I had before for what was great and enrapturing, and I kept coming across wonders and creations that made the separation easier for me to bear. An enigmatic whiff of the east, an atmosphere of barrenness, sadness, and hunger over objects and vistas gave the landscape a more potent force, and dreams and intimations supplemented the strange reality. Away in the east, the advance was continuing. That was all we were told.

In spite of that, our lives were changing too, and while wartime existence might make us skeptical about our souls, we were trying to adopt attitudes, masks, and postures that would be equal to the demands and conditions of what lay ahead. So each of us went within himself in his own way and mastered step-by-step his preparation.

At first there was the primordial circling around God. But the idea of God paled against the promise of destiny. I didn't want to be a weakling and lean against his omnipresence in my fear and need, not leave my happiness and sorrow in his fatherly hands, accept my lot as punishment and mercy, and console myself with his sacraments and promises. With rare logic, I didn't want to recognize any commands that, as a soldier, I would be unable to observe, and I told myself even then that I wasn't responsible for anything that I lived, thought, or said as a soldier, whether it was wisdom, experience, love, or death. My cosmos was now populated by angels and demons, and Jesus to me became more and more a prophet and less and less the Son of God.

But in a world without God, there had to be new forces that determined my standpoint and rooted my spiritual life.

The shivers of preparation blew through me, and all unknowing, I stepped into a heroic nihilism. Or so I thought.

Life was suffering. Death ruled the world. After the pain of birth, man's path led through sweat, anxiety, grief, fear, and hunger. Death was the only release; it took destruction to restore freedom and peace. It was a terrible thing to live in this world, in meaninglessness, viciousness, and godlessness. Better, as the Greeks said, never to have been born. The Flood and the end of the world were the only consolation; destruction was the final task of the seer and expert of our age. The last gods still needed to be forgotten, the idols smashed, love eradicated, procreation foiled, and life concluded. Ruins, dirt, and ashes should lie there as plainly visible, as they had long secretly been forming the picture of the world. But to the living, it was not only a matter of being in this void without metaphysical shelter—in doom and dread, bitter irony and dance of death, laughter and torture. It was tolerating its frightfulness, and also to want this fiendish life as it was, to take it as it came, and to love it in its barren bitterness and corruption, to call it beautiful, and to live it powerfully to the end; to find pride in its gruesomeness, delight in its decay, enthusiasm in its devastation; to deepen the worst horror with one's intellect, to live consciously and die coolly, at one with a reviled fate. There was merely the brazen inexorable necessity, Ananke, going her ways, over men and times as over grass and sand, grinding everything under her heel and at the same time alerting it all to a meaningless and godless existence. She tossed the church and the atom on a pair of scales, despised God and glorified death, and still bore fruitful blossoms in her soul: nightshade growth of time.

Only war could breed these thoughts, and they remained there, through all its phases and guises. In every crisis, it is to them the adventurer returns; from their humus his inner fate nourishes itself. My circling around God became an erring around death and void. There was no other way. I hoped, and I carried my stars, but they shone with a different light.

That was the spirit in which I wanted to go to war. I loved life because it was cruel in its beauty, appalling in its goodness, deadly in its fruitfulness, because our existence was a tragedy; birth, condemnation, and death were a liberating curse. I demanded roughness and danger to test myself in, a day full of toil and bitterness in which to purify myself. What I wanted was a transformation beyond consolation, dream, and refuge with God; and I found my pride and my greatness in wanting this carnival of killing and burning just exactly as it was; and to love it, and to stand in it without illusion, support, or belief; to laugh into the void and still be there, in the criminal pleasure of being cut adrift from gods and angels. I wanted despair for myself, and wounds, that I might survive them, and I felt strong enough to take up the fight with scorn, hunger, and rage. And perhaps all that was just the demented mask of man, who in the limbo of his destiny finds himself breaking down. I was given all the things I dreamed of. But I did not pass their test. I still needed to ripen to my fate.

The Indian summer faded away, autumn arrived, and the levels of the San rose. The bridge at Jaroslaw, dynamited during the fighting against Poland and now half repaired, was at risk. The river tore away supports and embankments; beams washed down the stream; the levee was undermined, and parts of it were collapsing.

We marched there in a fine rain, to salvage lumber, support what was still standing, and keep watch on the levee. On the horizon, Jaroslaw disappeared in haze and rain dust. Meadows, sodden pastures, groups of trees, and huts passed by. We reached the river at noon. Storm clouds, darkness, and rainbows menaced to the west; colorless sunshine trickled down onto the fields. The broad grassy banks had disappeared under a murk of clay-colored and dirty gray water; only bushes stuck out, collecting scummy bubbles in the mesh of their twigs. The spirit of the eastern landscape wafted toward us: melancholy, emptiness, expanse, a twilit mood, and as if to order, the remnants of the bridge obtruded into the oppressive scene of abandon and strangeness. Now I knew how far away I was from home. An unwelcoming country took me in, where I could not live, only die, or, like Ahasuerus, wander forever, a drifter, evicted, a ghostly shadow, an exile, wafted about by the choirs of the dead and the night wind off the hills, consumed by spirits and as lonely as at the edge of the world. The only way a man could live here was in tents, take them down, set them up, take them down again, always on the road in no-man's-land. And only the grave would set an end to yearning and suffering, fear and abandonment. Any notion of becoming had to be a grave error here; there was no adventure, no romance, not here. Only the year governed with its wheel of perpetual return; the soul lost its features, the wanderer his mask and his face. And so I entered the demesne of my new life, staggering from one contradiction to the next.

We got to work. From barges and rafts we laid new foundations, attached drifting timbers, anchored what was left of the props, spanned wires, and dragged earth and stones into the dikes. We scooted fearlessly around in the rapids, whirlpools, and foam. And by evening the bridge had been saved.

Railwaymen played host to us, and for the first time in a while we ate our fill. The moon dipped land and water in its unreal light, and I breathed in the cool air as a portent of a better, finer life to come.

My notions of the future expanded. I had intimations and dreams. I felt curiosity, an appetite for novelty, for the strange and extraordinary, which kept returning and pulling life forward. Panic alternated with a bizarre pleasure in everything that went against me and seemed to mock me. I wanted the plumb opposite, the improbable, the impossible that didn't belong to me, and in this desire marked the beginning of the view by which everything was pure adventure, in either thought or experience. I drifted. I had let myself drop into the stream, and now I was waiting to see which plank would come along and rescue me, which skiff would pick me up, which coast would permit me to land. I referred to this as my passive adventurism: getting tangled up in dangerous and dicey situations and waiting to see how the knot might be unpicked.

Uncertainty, unfamiliarity, the imminent, the untrodden refused to allow any durable form to appear. A state of readiness was the most that might be expected.

New orders came, and we traveled on. I wasn't sorry to take my leave of the limbo, the way station of Jaroslaw.

Monotonous, mournfully beautiful country went past. Indian summer baked the fields, veils of trees and shrubs flamed in russet glory, and the grass withered. The sun rose in infinite silence and loneliness over seas of fog. Scattered farmhouses loomed up out of the distance. Ruined bridges and houses told of the progress of the war. The fields ran on endlessly; villages stretched along the hills; children minded the farm animals. Roads led away into the distance, straight, straight, straight. Autumn dropped ever sadder colors onto the melancholy palette. Villages looked deserted, people like dream figures in a shadowy existence—as if, though long dead, they were still doing their work, under some mystical compulsion.

We got off at Fastov. I said goodbye to the train, and to everything I had ever known. The candle had burned down to a stump; it was like saying goodbye to life itself.

Russian Passion

Russia. Now the war began for us as well, and it was as though we were merely the latest to be involved in the ongoing crucifixion of Russia and its people. We saw only women and old people; the men had fled or gone into hiding. But even if we didn't believe everything the muzhiks told us, we knew, and we could see for ourselves and hear it and feel it wherever we went, that this people of so many mingled races had always suffered, that all through history its roads had been a *via crucis* that hadn't even merited a martyr's crown. Nor did we either, because we were cowardly before the law. Not only self-division, despair, humiliation, brutality, abjectness, rue, and bruising, as the poets say, constituted this suffering. The peasant in his poverty, in misery, degeneration, and slothful passivity, was condemned to idiocy and servitude: He bore his mute animal suffering under the czar, the knout of the landowner, and in the collective farm. He suffered from the climate, was duped, beaten, was raw material, learned to be cunning and cruel himself, and still suffered on into eternity. He stood on the bridge between Asia and Europe, in the twilight, on the everlasting Good Friday, and a hundred generations had only one face among them.

We saw the hunger and the misery, and under the compulsion of war, we added to it. The Passion took us into its territory. We marched.

Fastov. A vast plain unfolded outside the railway station, and the paved road led dead straight over low hills and fields. Straight, dead straight, that was the theme of Russia. Fields, corn stubble, and meadows slid past; only very rarely a tree or a house on the horizon. The sun glared; dust whirled up. We carried our packs and rifles and marched in loose file under their weight. At the very first rest stop, we sprawled onto the dusty grass at the side of the road, staggered up on the command to continue marching, and dragged ourselves onward. I started to fall behind. As evening fell, I would pass comrades insensible on the roadside, felled by heatstroke or exhaustion. A little troupe of us moved into a village, were allocated a barn, and lay down. We couldn't eat, barely drank, and slept in leaden fatigue.

In the morning, trucks came and saved us the agonizing march. We rode to Kiev, were put with regiments of the 95th Infantry Division, the 14th Company of the 279th Infantry Regiment. And there I remained for the war. There my road began into the Russian Passion.

We spent one more night in Kiev. In the morning, before it was light, we set out and stood shivering on the road. For a long time progress was stalled at the bridge over the Dnieper. A keen wind blew off the river. Finally our columns moved across. Horses pulled the artillery pieces; a munitions cart with blankets and equipment, knapsacks and booty, traveled with each light antitank gun. At noon, while we rested, the field kitchen drove past the ranks and gave out food; the supply column was a long way back. The front was an unknown distance ahead. We heard that our motorized units were pursuing the Russians. That was all we knew, no names of places or directions. At night we set up tents or slept in houses, lying on straw and always tired.

Slowly but irresistibly we moved across the steppe toward the great adventure. Sun seared. Dust and sweat begrimed our faces, and the march and the road seemed never-ending. Low white-washed cottages stood among fruit trees and wells, all of it lost in infinitude. Women in brightly colored headscarfs stood barefoot on the broad road, beautiful figures among them. We saw hardly any men. We marched.

Our feet swelled up and hurt; our breaths came quicker and shallower till we were allowed to rest. Every night was a relief. I felt an utter stranger in Russia.

We were given a day's respite. A white village in the midst of apples and poplars took us in. We could wash and sleep, wash our clothes, and fix something to eat with stolen eggs and flour. There were occasional beautiful simple houses standing in the bare landscape. But mostly they were squat, ugly huts, in which four or six or ten people lived in a single small, low-ceilinged room. They were beam constructions, with daub walls, the cracks stuffed with moss, the inside roughly painted, the outside generally not. Their roofs were straw. A stamped earthen floor supported the great stove on which the inhabitants slept. Mice rustled in the straw and dust. There was a bench, a table, and occasionally a bed or pallet by the stove. Underneath it quivered rabbits, pigs, and the vermin that would attack us. Bedbugs bothered us at night, fleas broke our rest, and lice multiplied in our uniforms. Spiders, flies, wood lice, and cockroaches scuttled over the tables and over our faces and hands. The illumination was provided by an oil lamp. Sometimes after our arrival, the women would have lit the candle in front of the icon and pulled a Bible out of its hiding place and laid it on a little corner table, with artificial flowers. Above it were pictures of the Madonna and various saints, prints mounted on gold paper and framed in wooden boxes. Some of the women wore crosses on chains around their necks and crossed themselves before meals. Otherwise they passed their time in sleep and idleness. The winter was empty, and there was little to do in the autumn. They lived on potatoes and sour black bread, usually kept a few chickens or geese, sometimes a pig or a cow. But they were strong and healthy. This was what they were used to, this was their life from day to day, and neglect, squalor, and poverty bothered them little.

We marched on.

Rain streamed down. We slithered over grass and clay, and the roads turned to bog. Snow and hail were carried on the wind. Winter set in at the beginning of October. The roads were bottomless, and we marched on from village to village. In Glukhov we stopped for a day, we slept in Kutok, and yet we had no idea where we were.

Fate drove us on, and we didn't know where we were going till we got there. We were not called upon to fight, the enemy was still far distant, but the march alone was sufficiently bitter for us. We crept on through the mud. Our artillery pieces and munitions carts bogged down; the horses broke down, were barely capable of pulling light loads. The supply column was delayed; we were no longer victualed. One after another, the horses collapsed and died or had to be put out of their misery. We replaced them with tougher Russian ponies, which we managed to capture wild or took away from collective farms. They in turn starved, became scrawny and weak, the bones stuck out of their worn, untended hides.

Our coats and blankets grew wet and moldy, had clumps of clay on them, and we could no longer get our sodden boots off our swollen, inflamed feet. The dirt and the lice gave us sores. But we marched—stumbling, reeling—pushed the carts out of the muck, and tramped on dully through showers of rain, sleet, and occasional night frosts.

Finally there was a little forest after the desolate plain, a few pines, beeches, alder scrub, not more. Beyond it the flat expanse began again. We spent the night with farmers who had been German prisoners in World War I. They were friendly and hospitable and complained about the new age in their country. But we could not make any comparisons.

Frost-reddened maples and lofty birches with their last yellow leaves stood in a dusting of snow. We hardly saw the beauty of the enchanting scenes. We were hungry. The cooks slaughtered cattle and pigs on the way and requisitioned peas, beans, and cucumbers everywhere. But a little midday soup wasn't enough to get us through our exertions. So we started taking the last piece of bread from women and children, had chickens and geese prepared for us, pocketed their small supplies of butter and lard, weighed down our vehicles with flitches of bacon and flour from the larders, drank the overrich milk, and cooked and roasted on their stoves, stole honey from the collective farms, came upon stashes of eggs, and weren't bothered by tears, hand wringings, and curses. We were the victors. War excused our thefts, encouraged cruelty, and the need to survive didn't go around getting permission from conscience. Women and children were made to go to the wells for us, water our horses, watch our fires, and peel our potatoes. We used their straw for our horses or for bedding for ourselves, or else we drove them out of their beds and stretched out on their stoves.

The country started to get hilly. The villages got still more wretched, and the mud got worse. Men and horses were at the end of their strength. The trucks and tanks of the lead units got stuck in the mire. The advance faltered. We moved into a village and rested. Slowly we recovered. We suffered from diarrhea. Our bellies were a ferment of swamp. We were disgusted and appalled, but we couldn't fast. Hunger hurt too much.

We moved in semipermanently. We drove the women out of their homes and pushed them into the most wretched of the dwellings. Pregnant or blind, they all had to go. Crippled children we shooed out into the rain, and some were left with nothing better than a barn or shed, where they lay down with our horses. We cleaned the rooms, and heated them, and looked after ourselves. We always managed to find potatoes, fat, and bread. We smoked makhorka, the heavy Russian tobacco. Otherwise we lived as well as we could and didn't think about the deprivation that would come after us. Kosmomolemyanskoye was the name of the village.

I fell into homesickness and pining. The extent of my life and thoughts never got beyond tiredness, fantasies of desertion, need for sleep, hunger, and cold. My star went on its predestined way. Beyond all love, I drifted in my Russian Passion. That I had once walked by the sea in a storm, that I had lived and dreamed: That seemed itself like a dream. I would give up God and my own humanity for a piece of bread. I had no comrades. Everyone fended for himself, hated anyone who found better booty than himself, wouldn't share, would only trade, and tried to get the better of the other. There was no conversation beyond the day-to-day. The weaker was exploited, the helpless left in his misery. I was deeply disappointed, but then I too had become hard.

We froze. At first there was a thin layer of snow on the road, but as it grew colder, the paths slowly became firmer. We were able to start marching again. At Fatesh, there was a thaw, and we were knee-deep in the soft sludge again. Then we froze, but there was no winter clothing to be had. Any woolen garments we found became ours. Blankets, scarfs, pullovers, shirts, and especially gloves we made off with at any opportunity. We pulled the boots off the old men and women on the street if ours were wanting. The torture of the marches embittered us to the point that we became impervious to the sufferings of others. We showed off our ill-gotten gains and with the impression we made with a pistol on a defenseless woman, who by ill fortune was a Russian.

We were oblivious to the way we were often given food when we set foot in a hut, to the peasants giving us their makhorka to smoke, a woman freely offering us a couple of eggs, or a girl sharing her milk with us. We still dug around in every corner, even if we let what we had taken just go bad later. We didn't want it; it was a sort of compulsion. Our commands kept telling us that we were the lords of the universe, in a conquered country. We had to go on; the front was still far off. No one asked us how we did it. Our legs ran with pus, the socks rotted on our feet, lice owned us, we were cold, hungry, ill with diarrhea, scabies, diphtheria, jaundice, and kidney infections, we dragged ourselves forward on sticks, rode bareback on horses, or gripped the sides of carts with frozen fingers, but we marched on.

Another village, another one of the innumerable villages we saw, and whose names we heard only to forget them immediately afterward. We got there in the dark and slept in a barn. A stove burned, but it gave no warmth. The straw was wet; our coats and boots were heavy. We lay down, freezing, trembling with cold, exhaustion, and rage. In the morning we moved into a house where an infant had just died. The women were wailing over the small white corpse in a long, drawn-out, free-form lament. The father kissed the bare hands, the bloodless lips. They were weeping, but they gave us their hospitality freely and kindly. There was no doctor anywhere about, so I wrote out the death certificate. The old farmer thanked me. He talked about his life, long years as a prisoner in Siberia, in chains, the bitter cold, with forced labor and beatings. We never learned what his crime had been; nothing but humility and kindness shone from his pale blue eyes.

The carpenter put together the coffin from unfinished boards in the yard. The women, singing again, dressed the boy in his Sunday best, bedded him on hay, pressed a cross nailed together from a couple of sticks in his folded hands. They buried the coffin in their garden. No cross marked it, just a brown tump in the bleak landscape. Parents, brothers and sisters, and friends ate a chicken for a funeral feast. One was cooked for us as well. The hospitality was extraordinary. We didn't deserve it.

Kursk. We barely saw it. We did nothing but go through the buildings for food and woolen garments. Working Russian prisoners we stole bundles and tobacco from. We smoked greedily and at last lay down warm and peaceful.

In a village beyond Kursk we had more peace. A tiny consignment of winter clothing, blankets and headgear, a few gloves, arrived. It was in Budonovka. Reports reached us of fighting close at hand. We were almost at the front. We set up sentries in the snowy country and bitter cold, and some had their feet frozen. But we got mail, and in the quiet, our thoughts concentrated on our own lives. I read and wrote; I watched the sun rise and set over the snow. At night we kept vigils in the house. Outside, the frost jingled, the north wind went howling around the house, and the snow glittered under the stars. Then snow started falling again and covered the plain higher and denser. Everything in me became quiet. The firs loomed blackly on the railway embankment, and the land shone white and bluish brown in the moonlight. Meteorites fell.

But sometimes I would again be seized by apathy. We were

passive, without hope, without belief and refuge, and even the war seemed empty to us. Simple things retained their value, but everything great became an irrelevance to us. A stern, cruel necessity made us into the people the time required.

A patrol encountered the enemy. We set out, and with orders to take Shchigry, we left our Russian Passion and went into winter warfare.

The Winter War

THE ATTACK ON SHCHIGRY

We received our baptism of fire. For the first time we heard the whistling of mortars, the whipping of machine-gun bursts, the wild shrilling and bright brutal crash of shells. And it wasn't a game. Except for burned-down villages, hulks of tanks, graves, and the fires of Kursk on the rim of the sky, we hadn't seen anything of the real war. But even then our faces had sometimes turned to stone. Now, though, we saw men fall, saw blood and wounds, and we carried our rifles in our hands and fired them blindly into the empty space in front of us.

On the first day of the offensive we attacked a village. The remaining Russian defenders quickly withdrew. On the way I lost contact with my men. We left our vehicles at the edge of a ravine and found soldiers sitting in the snow, weeping. They had frozen feet, but still had to go on. A horse fell, and I led it. Finally I found the advance route and followed the footprints into the village, sat down freezing in a house, and was brought food. I didn't know there were Russian soldiers sleeping only a few houses away, who were woken by the shots of the attackers, which roused me as well.

The next morning we came under fire from a column of tanks and had to bury our heads in the snow. A yelled prayer went up to us to keep our discipline. We weren't praying for our lives; we called out for courage, to keep us strong and proud, and save us from cowardice. Cowardice was worse than death, and even a peaceable fellow like me despised anyone who trembled for his life and sought to avoid ruin. I loved to prove myself in danger. That was the ultimate meaning of those times. And in that chaos of primal fear and dread, the soul could come up with nothing but this final echo of childhood.

Our guns made no impression on the steel monster, but it still withdrew in the evening with the Russian troops. Around midnight we marched past burning farmhouses and smoking huts to a short, exhausted sleep in a village.

One soldier forced his way into a farmhouse, and the farmer set bread and milk before the hungry man. But the soldier wanted more. He wanted honey, which he soon found, and flour and lard. The farmer beseeched him, his wife cried, and in their fear of starving, the couple tried to wrest his booty away from him. The soldier smashed in the farmer's skull, shot the farmer's wife, and furiously torched the place. He fell that same night, hit by a stray bullet. But we shouldn't ask after God's justice in war.

On the next day the Russians put up fierce resistance. We had to fight every step of the way. I remained behind with a machine gun, guarding the supply column and the spare munitions against stray attackers. We spent endless hours in the ice and snow, with no protection against the biting wind, eating frozen honey from the comb, as we didn't have bread or water. We soon lost all feeling in our feet. Some suffered frozen toes, ears, and hands if they were carrying munitions chests, and failed to notice

the blood stopping in their hands, or were forced to lie motionless in the snow for hours while enemy fire shrilled over their
heads. We were bitter and irritable and then dull and indifferent. At last we moved off. A small hamlet had been conquered,
but the Russians had burned it all down before leaving. We
looked out bundles of straw, spread them out in a hollow, laid
canvas over them, crept completely under our blankets, and
pressed ourselves together. We slept in spite of our icy feet. But
whoever went out on sentry duty didn't dare lie down afterward,
because their foreheads were already sore, and some showed
signs of frostbite. We lit big fires, staggered and hopped around
the flames, and waited for day to break. The night was the color
of blood, from the fires in the villages around, and the hills
echoed darkly with the thunder of explosions. These experiences
made me feel a stranger to myself.

The order came to strike camp. We marched toward Shchigry, and took the first heights without having seen a single Russian. Again I stayed behind with a machine gun and a couple of
comrades, since we were unable to keep up, enfeebled as we
were by diarrhea and exhaustion. From up on the slopes we saw
the little town in the valley and rows of houses on the hills
around.

We lay in the snow with some men from another platoon.
Sporadic fire from Russian infantry weapons blew over our
heads. We might be hit at any moment. We were forced to wait
it out, unmoving, inert, unresisting, dead material.

Suddenly one of us leaped up. No one had given any order.
But we followed him, breathing easily again, once more con-
scious of our being there, not brave but in a frenzy, done in by
inactivity and waiting, driven by cold into a panic of movement,
courageous out of a fear of keeping still, and then suddenly trans-

ported by a blinding access of enthusiasm. Death and danger were forgotten; life was justified by mere action.

Men fell. The wounded screamed. We didn't pay them any regard. We charged like maniacs to the edge of the town. We didn't throw ourselves to the ground, not even when the machine-gun bullets whistled so close by us that we could feel them. The defenders were gunned down mercilessly, and whatever we saw of honey, fat, sugar, and good bread was hurriedly stowed away, while next door a brief firefight was still in progress, and our comrades were being slain.

The Russians fled. As night fell, we moved past burning factories and silos into Shchigry. Bridges burned and crashed, mortars continued to fire at us; we didn't care.

We lay down in a house, not bothering with sentries, and slept as though comatose.

The next day we looked at the wreckage. Debris, bricks, glass, and charred beams lay all over the road. Ruins everywhere. We declared a few days' rest.

Simple people were kind and hospitable to us that first night. They washed our shirts, brought out pillows and blankets for us to sleep on. We let it happen, gave ourselves to them in a limitless display of trust, and went around as in a dream. When we thought back to the fighting, we felt an unstable mixture of horror and disappointment. Fighting, danger, and nearness of death seemed to us like a dream of the inadequacy of war. It wasn't sufficiently shaking and enthusing, yet horror grinned at us from all around. We didn't know whether we had been hoping for a long siege, whether the swift victory offended us, or whether a secret horror informed us that it would have been better for us if we had died or been wounded. It wasn't the battle that caused the suffering, but the vicious cold, the helpless waiting around. Then, as if coming to our senses, we suddenly grasped the meanness all around us of dying and having to kill.

At that time I still got over things quickly. Individual details went under in a vast ocean of apathy and oppression and never took shape.

We moved in with a couple of young women, whom we called the Daughters of the World Revolution, who impressed us with their pride and their comradely attitude. It was as though they sensed a tie between us as coevals, some shared quality in our yearning and our fate that was stronger than the division between us that the war wrought. Strangely, there was an intimation here of a greater peace than any war could ever bring.

With our looted bread and honey, and their chickens and potatoes, we prepared a common feast and talked in a blithe mixture of languages.

Our last evening in Shchigry we spent with a landowning family, who were hanging on in a dismally converted building and had nothing left to remind them of prerevolutionary times beyond a photograph album. The old man, an upright, strong, and good-looking patriarch, brought in his daughters, simple, delicate girls who came in holding hands, as if to comfort one another in a dehumanized world, and thus cling to some paradisal youth. He began with an ironic rendition of the "Internationale" and followed it with a teary version of the czar's hymn, the "Stenka Razin," and some hymns. I spoke French with his wife. She spoke in low, shy tones. Her face was still beautiful but marked by suffering. I got to hear of the expropriation of landowners, of various forms of forced labor and increasing hardship. One son was in Siberia; another had been killed; the fate of a daughter married in Odessa remained unknown. We felt sorry for them. We did not yet understand that a new spirit and new growth were bound to trample on the precious things of the past.

Then we marched on to the assembly point on the river Tim. Many were sick, all were exhausted, and the marches in increasing cold became more arduous by the day. And now we were marching into the unknown. We crossed the small, frozen river, barely restored. Then endless marches across frozen snow, in icy winds, under the full moon, toward Volovo. Our objective was Voronezh. We never got there.

The day before we were to take Volovo, I overslept, along with a couple of comrades. No one woke us; everyone thought only of himself and his own hunger and exhaustion and the implacable orders that forced him to march on. The three of us followed the footprints across the featureless, measureless plain. We encountered Russian soldiers, who threw their guns down in the snow. We did nothing to them, as our uncertainty grew, and our strange lostness. In one village we saw Russian troops resting with their horses, watching us through their binoculars, but they didn't shoot at us and seemed at pains to give the impression of being prisoners.

And so we marched on, the very last stragglers, through Russian forces readying themselves for a counterstrike, to encircle our own rash undertaking.

That night we came to a village where we found our own unit again.

THE FLIGHT FROM VOLOVO

The soldiers squeezed out onto the jam-packed streets; horses and trucks, guns and carts, bunched together on the retreat from the first failed assault on Volovo. We never learned the name of the village, but no one forgot the place, and everyone knew what was meant by Nikolausdorf.

After midnight, just as we were getting off to sleep and feeling a little warmer, mounted Cossacks stormed through the village. They tossed hand grenades into the houses and were gone as soon as the alarm was given.

That night there were eight soldiers asleep in a house off on its own on the edge of the village that the Cossacks surrounded. They woke to the danger. Two of them jumped through the windows and died, each hit by several bullets. Two others sleepily got up as the Russians forced their way in, and were mowed down. Two more were taken prisoner in the hallway and were made to join the Cossacks in towing away the captured guns and to use them on us for months to come. One was up in the hayloft and got off with a nervous collapse. The last was hidden behind a cupboard. The Russians lit the room with matches but failed to see him. He too went mad, started running off back west, and was picked up in Riga, as he was getting on a goods train there. No one could understand how he had gotten so far, and he was no longer able to give any sort of account of it himself.

The following morning a soldier doled out boxes of hand grenades among a hundred captured Russian prisoners and shot the survivors with his submachine gun. We took up a decoy position outside Volovo, while another section conducted the actual assault. We peppered the nests of resistance with all the light and heavy infantry weapons we had, but the Russians didn't give an inch. We knelt or lay in the snow; our knees froze fast to the ground; ice formed between our coats and our tunics. We stamped on the ground to get feeling back in our feet. The men's skin froze onto the metal of their rifles, because few had usable gloves; bleeding scraps were torn off their hands, which froze over before the blood could flow. Many froze to death, and many others ran off in despair. Even on our way here, there had been casualties, and now the numbers of dead and wounded climbed.

Vainly we waited for the white flare that was the agreed signal that the others had fought their way into Volovo. Night came. We had waited seven hours. The last of us staggered to our feet under cover of darkness but promptly fell down, because our feet couldn't carry us. Some vomited. We crawled and staggered forward until the blood began to circulate again. Then we were ordered to retire, and under fire from Katyusha rockets, we made our way back to Nikolausdorf, hoping for sleep and warmth.

But once again the Cossacks galloped up after midnight, hid their horses unremarked in the gully, and attacked the outer houses of the village, where the aid station was. The sentries fled, and the wounded were murdered by the Siberian troops. We were roused by the alarm. Half-dressed soldiers, men in their shirts, in socks, barefoot, rushed past us in terror. A full moon lit their frantic, mindless flight.

A medic collected together a score of men who stayed behind with us. We were armed with rifles, a bazooka, and pistols. The expanse of the plain lay open in front of us, in the ghostly light of the moon, and across it charged the Cossacks with their wild "URRAH," like a band of ghosts toward our group. In the fire of our rifles and our one gun, an attack of some four hundred Russians faltered. The survivors withdrew, but before we knew what was happening, they had outflanked us. We were surrounded.

Hand grenades went up in our midst. Several men fell, wallowed about on the snow with ripped-open bellies, got themselves tangled up in their own intestines. We broke up into smaller groups and laid into the drunken attackers with rifle butts; two of us were slit apart by bayonet thrusts. In pairs we stood by the corner of a barn, the medic still with us, while ten feet in front of us, the Russians oozed up out of the night like phantoms of death. My comrade fell. I lay in the snow and didn't shoot. It wasn't that my rifle was jammed, but at that time I was unable to shoot at men who were trying to kill me; I would sooner have died. That was the only hour of trial by fire in that winter campaign. The doctor meanwhile was potting attackers with his pistol.

The last of them melted away. We could still hear the chilling "URRAH" in the distance. The next time they charged across the plain, several of us fled. The Russians surged past us and gave chase, and they didn't come back. We seven survivors were left alone for a long time. The ordeal was over.

All through that night, fugitives kept returning. Men who had hidden somewhere, or kept running, and at their wits' ends now came back without knowing whether the Russians had taken the village or not. St. Nicholas's Day. Most had fresh frostbite; wounded men dragged themselves along. We kept watch among the corpses. The fat face of the moon stared down on the corpses in the snow. Contorted features, calm faces, dull, staring eyes, smashed skulls, slit bellies, squirts of blood and brains came to light as day broke. We went around ashen-faced, like dead men.

Then, almost without a fight, we marched into Volovo, demanding food, warmth, sleep. The buildings were partly on fire; Katyusha rockets were being fired at us. But we found only a few isolated Red Army soldiers in the buildings. They were shot. An order had been given not to take any prisoners. In one house we came upon some hot noodle soup, which the Russians had simply left. We sat down on the benches, propped our freezing feet on the bodies, and ate hungrily, without thinking about death and danger. In the pockets of the dead, we found bread and sugar, and we ate our fill. We weren't fastidious anymore.

In the evening there was an agitated command to leave right away. We had to try to slip the noose that a vast preponderance of Russian forces had almost drawn around us. The march back began without our having gotten any sleep, mute, in an unexpressed despair, just like the beginning of this tragedy of an ambitious advance into no-man's-land.

The moonlight shone down on the silent column of fugitives slowly making their way through the snow, reeling, slithering, stumbling westward. Ahead of us was uncertainty, perhaps no-man's-land, perhaps the enemy; behind us, certainly, the pursuing Russians. We were dog-tired on this third night without sleep. If there was a delay anywhere of a few minutes, we would already be leaning against the guns asleep, till the horses began to pull and we lurched awake. Then a swarm of men in camouflage dress surged toward us. Within seconds we had our machine gun set up, lashing bursts into the group. Some fell; the first of them were in front of us—German steel helmets, our own. There hadn't been many dead. We piled the worst of the wounded on carts, and they died on the way. No one bothered about the bodies. We staggered on. Even as we marched, we were overmanned by sleep. Our eyes closed, our legs went mechanically on; then our knees went, and we keeled over, awakened by pain, by the fall, pulled ourselves together, knelt, someone helped us to our feet, and with the last strength lent us by the fear of death, we tottered on. Any rest spelled death, we were told. The Russians are coming! That call worked like the crack of a whip: On! Silent, in despair, bitter, dull-witted, ghostly, we hurried westward like shades. We radioed for help, but no one could help us where we were. Several more men collapsed. They refused to get up and stayed where they lay. We kicked out at them, prodded them with rifles. Unhappily, with empty eyes, they got up. And marched on. Whoever was at the rear received no such assistance. He would freeze or be found and beaten to death.

Finally there was a rest period. One hour. It was in a tiny village. Along with many other soldiers, I slunk into a house and collapsed in a corner. I was asleep before I touched the floor. When I awoke, I was all alone. I'd been forgotten about, but my strength had returned. I slipped off the safety catch on my rifle and dashed outside. There was no one, neither friend nor foe. I hurried up a hill, and there saw my comrades in the distance, tiny dots in the snowscape. I set off after them. Hours went by, and then I caught up with them. My guardian angel hadn't abandoned me.

Russian planes bombed and strafed us. But at noon we rested in hard, dry winter sunlight in a village on the Kshen and slept.

It began to thaw. Our fighters and bombers smashed the ring, pounded the Russian troop concentrations. We greeted them with shouts of jubilation, tears in our eyes. Saved, provisionally, conditionally saved. Mercy for a while. Our Advent began.

ADVENT

The retreat faltered. We had no maps and didn't know the roads and the terrain. We had intended to winter behind the line of the river Tim, but we weren't there yet. We moved into another village, and that same night we received an order for twenty of us and a bazooka to come to the aid of a beleaguered outpost.

The outpost was in a railway crossing cottage, on the line from Livny to Kursk, situated three and four kilometers respectively from the nearest village and pillbox to the north and south of us. We had our antitank gun, two heavy and three light machine guns, and plenty of ammunition. We slept on hay spread over boxes of bullets and grenades. We had a stove for warmth and a rifle oil lamp for light. But that was pretty much all we had. We burned the fencing and finally the flooring. For twelve days we lived on potatoes, which we boiled with a little salt. We found some green makhorka to smoke, or we made do with hay. We drank snowmelt. There was no soap, and each of us had just one thin blanket. Tangled hair and beards, black hands, and most of us either festering and frostbitten or eaten alive by lice, scabies, and the inflammations on our legs. When we went out to do sentry duty, we wrapped ourselves in our threadbare blankets, but our icy feet drove tears of pain and rage to our eyes.

Over two days and three nights we were under continuous attack from the Russians, shelled by their artillery, or their infantry loomed up out of the fog, where either we killed them or they melted back into the night. Storm artillery afforded us some relief, but the lightly wounded had to stay where they were. Eleven men died or were badly wounded, three more lightly, two went over to the Russians, and one mutilated himself. Of thirty men in all. The gun had no more ammunition, and the machine guns had to economize. A concerted attack would have spelled the end of us, and we couldn't understand the enemy. Our doomed clutch of men melted away.

Advent for the doomed. We had to bear it; how we got through, no one bothered to ask. Our conversations revolved around relief—the perpetual delusion—and around home and flight. Bitterly we contemplated hunger, cold, need, and our disappearing position. We were all sick and irritable. Outbursts of rage and hate, envy, fistfights, sarcasm and mockery stood in for whatever might have remained of comradeship. Even if no one talked about danger and proximity of death anymore, they were still there. We didn't attend to our dead and didn't bury them either, just put on their coats and gloves. Things and values changed. Money had become meaningless. We used paper money for rolling cigarettes or gambled it away indifferently. Several got so far into debt that they couldn't pay with a year of their soldiers' wages, and that wouldn't be called in either. A piece of bread, though, was a fantasy that could not possibly be realized. But that too was part of the war. Death brought with it a limitless desire for sleep and oblivion. Only a few sought intimacy, most drugged themselves with superficialities, with gambling, cruelty, hatred, or they masturbated. This between fighting.

One night I was on sentry duty and saw the village burning in the distance. The snowfields were under fog. Then I saw a long line of Russians crossing the railway line, silhouetted against the fire, vague shapes in the night and fog. I couldn't raise the alarm or fire at them. The eerie spectacle captivated and silenced me. By the time someone else woke those within, they had already moved on.

Departure on Christmas Eve, as it got light. On the way we torched all the villages we passed through and blew up the stoves. We had been ordered to spread devastation, so that our pursuers could find no shelter. We obeyed, and our self-loathing overpowered even our joy at being released. Women wailed, children froze in the snow, and curses followed us. Soon we stopped asking. When we were issued a supply of cigarettes, we lit them at the burning houses. Then we marched dully and feebly on our way, holding on to the carts, and reached Arinok, a village on the river Tim.

The New Year began. Advent continued. There was nothing beyond the barest self-preservation. That was all that got us through so much cold and so many marches and sleepless nights.

Never had I sensed and affirmed the will to live so strongly as now. Life was a balancing act, a rope suspended over death. Sometimes we were befallen by a kind of crying without tears.

THE NEW YEAR

Arinok on the river Tim. At the beginning of the year we experienced the lowest temperatures of the entire winter campaign. We had to post sentries and spell each other every half hour. Our house was a long way from the last street; it was almost by the river. In front of us, the plain stretched away with occasional sparse cover. Day and night we got no rest, even if the Russians weren't attacking us. One sentry who collapsed in a haystack and carried on sleeping was court-martialed and shot. Another was unable to find the unit to which he was taking a message in the darkness and was sentenced to death for cowardice in the face of the enemy. Whoever stole food, even a piece of bread, was executed for looting. It was a tense time. Prisoners of war dangled off the trees all around, as a result of a command that was intended to frighten off the Russians. The war had become insane; it was all murder, never mind whom it affected. Rebellion was discouraged by fear of the enemy, who could no more be bothered with prisoners.

There was little food, and the bad quarters couldn't get warm. Our existence was one long complaint against the war. But no God took us under his wing. The couple of hours' rest we got at a time we spent sleeping on the stove. Lice multiplied, and the dirt and disease increased. No one avoided pyoderma and lymph inflammations. But only those who were already suffering from bone caries were sent to the hospital. Frostbite festered and stank in the heat of the stove. There was no lint. The same bandage, pus-encrusted and stiff with scabs and rotted flesh, was used again and again. We had to go easy on salves and ointments. Some had long rags of blackened flesh hanging off their feet. It was snipped off. The bones were exposed, but with their feet wrapped in cloths and sacking, the men had to go on standing sentry and fighting.

We had no winter clothing and never really got warm. Our perpetually cold feet hurt. Every footfall hurt, but we had to walk and move around. Frostbite could be interpreted as attempted self-mutilation. Our chilled guts couldn't deal with food. Everyone had diarrhea, and some had diphtheria. One was so enfeebled that he broke down on his way to the doctor and froze to death. Older men developed rheumatism and often screamed with pain. But we couldn't let anyone go.

I got lumbago and was moved back to the second village street, referred to as the support line. There I lay three days and nights on a stove, unable to sleep for pain. The following night I heard shots and cries, the "URRAH" of the Russians, and I crept out on all fours. The fighting went on for four hours. I sat in the house and wondered what was going to happen. I didn't care either way. Fleeing soldiers came in. They held their hands against the stove and rubbed their feet with snow to avoid frostbite at the very last moment. They propped me up until my limbs relaxed and I was able to walk again. We fled to Dubrovka.

We left our cannons behind, and threw away our machine guns. We left our blankets, bread sacks, mess tins, water bottles, and the recently arrived Christmas mail to the victors.

Dubrovka. We moved into new positions. A house with snowbanks in front of it and some straw was our strongpoint. On our flight there we ran into a fighting unit that had been on the run for a long time and had only just joined our lines again.

They had a few men, and hardly rested, some of them now turned around. They found their missing in the ruins of a village; they had fallen asleep in the snow and frozen to death. Others had crept into stoves and, with their frozen limbs, were unable to get out. The stoves had to be smashed up, and the lamenting casualties loaded on sleighs. In the field hospitals their arms and legs were amputated, and they died in the course of the operations.

It was garrison warfare. The front, such as it was, was a chain of widely separated villages. The Russians were able to march through in between us and pressed forward as far as Shchigry. We didn't know.

We found food. There were potatoes in cellars and bunkers, and we slaughtered sheep and cattle. But when the daily ration was four slices of bread, potatoes and slaughtering were banned, so as to build up a stock of provisions for the flood season ahead. We went on starving, and our guts and bellies didn't heal. Every day there were several hours of duty in the open, weapon cleaning also, but we had to collect our own wood and provisions. We waited a month for mail.

The Russians attacked Dubrovka. They came at night. We put up no resistance, because fighting, sacrifice, and war, none of it mattered anymore. A remnant of us fled across the plain to Belaya. Tanks approached us. We tied camouflage tunics to our rifles, swung them about, and surrendered. But they were German tanks. We were forced to climb aboard. We rode back to Dubrovka, retook it, and the Russians suffered heavy casualties. Another group of refugees was targeted by our artillery and suffered losses.

Our quarters were wrecked, and there were corpses littered about everywhere. We covered the German dead with tarpaulins; with the Cossacks we took off their felt boots and caps, as well as their pants and underpants, and put them on. We now moved closer together in the few houses still standing. One soldier had been unable to find any felt boots, which were an excellent protection against the cold. The next day he found a Red Army corpse frozen stiff. He tugged at his legs, but in vain. He grabbed an ax and took the man off at the thighs. Fragments of flesh flew everywhere. He bundled the two stumps under his arm and set them down in the oven, next to our lunch. By the time the potatoes were done, the legs were thawed out, and he pulled on the bloody felt boots. Having the dead meat next to our food bothered us as little as if someone had wrapped his frostbite between meals or cracked lice.

The dead lay where they lay. After weeks they were collected on sleighs, piled up in ruined houses along with horse cadavers, doused with gasoline, and lit.

Otherwise every day passed in the same way, in the drab monotony of sentry duty, scraps of sleep, worries about food and fuel, and the other duties we had to do. We had grown poor. Finally blankets started to arrive in ones and twos, and other essential equipment. I was crazy with homesickness and fatigue, and standing sentry in the terrible cold, I suffered a nervous collapse, fired at shadows, and ended up being found exhausted and unconscious in the blizzard by the man who relieved me. Saved. After that crisis, I quickly got better and recovered my confidence and will to live. The horror that clung on to despair and exalted itself into a cynical-heroical yes, this demented affirmation of doom: That was the greatness of the men in Russia and the suicide of the soul.

We stood guard over the Dubrovka gorge, looking like ghosts, midway between corpses and hanged men. The moon was crescent, the cold was preparing for one final assault, but the enemy was quiet.

I wanted to forget, to forget everything, merely in order to remain human. In that spirit I wrote everything down in my diaries, in order to slough it off and shed it for good. It didn't work. I had gotten to know only one side of Russia, the ruined churches and wintertime. And yet I believed that this war had to be, to prepare for some future as yet unknown, and I lost myself in bizarre fantasies. My purulent legs made me unfit to serve. I was driven back to the supply column and received treatment there.

That was the end of the winter campaign so far as I was concerned. I had been saved at the last moment. But I was lost.

Return Home

Fate did with me as it pleased. I understood how little I was able to affect it by anything I thought or did and reserved the freedom to give of my best only when things were at their worst. But I lived on the edge. Death, the blind strangler, had failed to find me, but a human being had died in Russia, and I didn't know who it was.

Thinking despairing thoughts, I lay on the pallet, my purulent leg swollen and braced. I was in safety with the supply column, yet I was unhappier than ever. I was in pain. I didn't get better, and after the third inspection the doctor sent me to the hospital.

I packed together my last few things, a wooden spoon, a Russian knife, and the bread sack of a dead Cossack, and was taken on a sleigh to the principal aid station, was bandaged up, and was sent to a house to spend the night.

A heavily wounded man was delivered, unconscious, with shrapnel in his chest and head. He had been supposed dead and was bandaged only after lying out in the frost for several hours. It was too late. He lay groaning on the thin straw. His hands, brown with frozen blood, were scratching away at his bandage, making jerky movements in shadows and candlelight. I sat down beside him and took his restless, desperate hands in mine. It was a struggle against his blind, unconscious energies. Once he broke loose and stared at me with sightless eyes. His ghostly hand gestured at my chest, as if blaming me for his suffering and death. Horror gripped me, and he fell back and died. But I couldn't find any rest. I kept seeing his accusing hand, the appalled eyes of the dying man staring at me. I was a soldier too and so partly responsible for his plight.

At daybreak, a sleigh transported me to the nearest aid station, a cold, gloomy building where casualties writhed like helpless worms on the thin straw. Volyhnian fever. Their groans and cries blew through my dreams. I got up and went outside. The night wind sang in the trees. The fact that I was sick and was allowed to sleep felt like a comfort. All I wanted was to rest. Soon my fate summoned me back to suffering and action.

Driven by sleigh to Malo-arkhangelsk. Under several blankets, we lay in harsh frost and froze. On by truck to Ponyri. Then joined a Russian hospital train. A coal fire glowed; the others told their stories. I lay there, half asleep, wholly apathetic, and allowed everything to be done to me. I was just a shuttlecock of the powers.

At Orel station there was another train waiting. We boarded that. I sat in the compartment blankly. When I heard this one was going as far as Warsaw, I wept.

Day after day, night after night, the train trundled through the white winterland. Bryansk. Smolensk. Minsk. Steps home. In Ostroleka Mazowieckie, we were taken off and joined a casualty clearing station. We were deloused, bathed, given fresh clothes, and suddenly found ourselves lying in white cotton sheets, no longer having to freeze, to starve, to go out on sentry duty. We could sleep, were tended, and we couldn't understand it. It was like a dream. We had supposed there was only ice and snow in the world and, in a sudden fear of anything kind and beautiful, found ourselves assailed by homesickness for Russia. We longed for the white winter hell, for pain, privation, danger. We didn't know what else to do with our lives. We were afraid to be home and now understood what the war had done to our souls.

I was able to sleep yet stayed awake far into the night, listening to music on the radio and letting the past months pass in review, half a year that felt like several decades' worth. Once more I experienced dreamlike visions of the attack on Shchigry, and the flight from Volovo, of Advent and the winter war. One night, after a soft trickle of jazz, I heard the opening of a Beethoven symphony, and in a breathless, ceremonial hearkening, I crossed the threshold of that life that lay permanently beyond the war.

And so my return home transpired.

But in my own life, there was as yet no space for what I had been through. I traveled out of the Polish winter into early spring at home, saw the woods and mountains that I loved and had dreamed of in the Russian plains, stood by the train window and breathed in the smell of fields, the fragrant meadows, and peace. In Frankfurt-am-Main my journey west ended. I lay in bed.

On Good Friday I wrote out the account of my first Russian adventure. But as I was looking around for an ending, I could find no other way than to have the narrator kill himself, since he had lived his life, hung on, and lost, as his star had decreed.

I read and reread my passionate accusation, but every word of it struck me as wrong. In histrionics, irony, bitterness, and uncertainty, the whole danger of the war once again became clear to me. But I was allowed only to curse, and to hate, and to pre-empt. I had to learn to say yes again, as I had intended in the period of heroic nihilism. It was the only way I could go on living.

It had to be.

The war could break a man, millions suffered and died, and no conquest or crusade was worth this criminal insanity. The war showed apocalyptic traits, and there I saw its cosmic necessity. I had experienced greatness and heroism: the death struggle of our men. But there was neither comradeship, willing sacrifice, fighting spirit, heroism, nor fulfillment of duty. No. But everyone died at the right time and had his own death. If many cried out for death in war, then war would have to be. And so I termed my homesickness for Russia the magnetic attraction of death.

Where the dead had their death, that last maturation of life, last fulfillment out of a split that no one saw, the last necessity, those survivors returning home had the equally absolute imperative for change. Shaken or enraptured by war, the godless man turned to prayer, the man of faith cursed his God, the devout buried his trust, the fool bethought himself, the wise man fled into superficial enjoyment, broke inside, and collected the bricks for a new vision of the world—and some such change also happened to me, even if I didn't understand it.

It had to be.

I thought on.

Stone, flower, and animal were as much an expression, as much a manifestation of the divinity as man, and so, to mankind a world war was the same as an earthquake to the mountain range, a hail shower to the seed, a blight to the beast, an event outside our power, a catastrophe, a cosmic occurrence. Equilibrium would be restored in whatever time came after this war.

Even if all words and pictures failed, what had happened in

me, this invisible and yet traumatically evident change, had to mean something. Otherwise I was lost.

And so I found salvation in the crazy notion of cosmic and human necessity, pushed into the twilight of the soul. But on Easter morning, a sad soldier with my wrecked life, I wandered among the crocuses, columbines, rain smell, and thrush song of the park.

Later I gave myself up to my memories. Scenes of youth, friendship, love, and wanderings by the sea slipped by me, a beautiful and painful film on the canvas of the soul. I embarked on long vinous conversations. I wrote a lot, read, and yet was unable to find any way into myself.

When I got home, the sense of an intermission between wanderings wouldn't let go of me. Happily and blithely as I lived, and grateful as I was to my destiny for this reprieve, my mysterious homesickness for Russia only grew.

And so I went out with new readiness, as soon as my new posting came through. I was a soldier, and until all the resources and gifts of peace and freedom became available to me again, it was only as a soldier that I could withstand the challenges of life. Carried and propped everywhere, I didn't need to be me.

Home.

Russian Voyage

EASTWARD HO!

With cheerful intuitions, I set off on my journey east and saw it as an adventure in which I was playing a tragicomic role. Neither the war nor Russia frightened or overwhelmed me anymore. Whatever I was unable to change couldn't oppress me, and so I awaited whatever the mighty and the powers had in mind for me.

We crossed the Russian border, into the Ukraine, a green, flowering, fertile landscape, as I never would have guessed it after that first bleak white winter. The villages nestled against the hills in picturesque idylls. On the meadows, the first crop of hay was drying, but the harvest was still a long way off, and the cherries were small and green.

We were headed into a Gypsy life. The train stopped everywhere. Goods trains, tracks, and stations made up our world. We rode in passenger carriages, slept soundly on benches and floors, and felt at home. Our conversations were about music and poetry, philosophy of life and freedom of will, and we had little parties with our wine.

Then we looked out over hills and endless fields again, rarely any wooded country. Prisoners worked on the tracks, and the often beautiful women, breaking stones and laying sleepers, reminded us painfully of our youth. Before long we saw our voyage as an excursion with plenty of picnics and were astonished at the beauty of the world that we were passing through, rocked like babies in our swaying carriages.

Tarnopol. I sat by the window and wrote. The others slept. Alone as only a solitary waking man among sleepers can be, I listened to their groans and snorts. Outside, the rain was trickling down, women wandered over a bridge, an old man begged for bread. Life went on in the gloaming, and I felt oddly disconnected from it.

The plains grew mightier, as if the hills had chosen to withdraw from the east, so that man could be alone on the wide surface, under the wide heavens, alone with God and himself, nowhere hemmed in and incredibly small in his mortality. The landscape enjoined pensiveness, without making one sad. Because it was summer, the earth was green, the sky was lofty and cloudy, and poppy, rape, and bindweed flowered everywhere.

I watched the country and made architectural and cultural notes. But what fascinated me, more than any of the structures and plans of the new order, was the Russian soil. It was like a vision to me. Weeds flourished, and crops flourished with them.

Thousands of years passed over the unaltered drip-drip of Russia. Unremarked, the hourglass dribbled its sand. The earth bowed to the law of seasons, blossomed and grew mightily in the summer, burned into fall, and passed into the drabness of the rainy season. Winter wrapped it in deep snow, and the frost hardened and melted seven times with the moon. But never did plains, hills, and woods change their aspect.

Man here was a stranger and a guest. He might plow and till the black earth, hack at the trees, sow and harvest for hundreds of years, but that didn't make him the master of this monstrous country and its spirits. He was not at home in the richness and beauty of the villages of the Ukraine, not in the clean places and woodlands of Ruthenia, not in the barrenness and poverty of the southern steppes, the northerly swamps and forests, or the giant cities he had planted as refuges for himself. He continued to dwell on the bridge between heaven and hell, as a nomad and a visitor. His fleeting time on earth disappeared among endurance, yearning, and readiness, and the generations came and went, with nothing to tell them apart, one from another.

The Golden Horde, Napoleon's march into uncertainty, the burning of Moscow, and the flight of the Corsican, the wars with Turkey, and the war with Japan had barely brushed the surface of the plain and had failed to give this land any history. The earth drank sweat, drank blood, swallowed up corpses, fields and forests thrived on the carcasses, and the burned villages returned. Timber was speedily felled and assembled with ax and hammer, and the houses were back in the landscape, hunched and cowed-looking, whitewashed, as though to hide from greatness and God. Only the churches with their onion domes, messengers from Greece and Byzantium, imprinted the landscapes, often with ugly cupolas. Christianity had affected the vision and the soul of the people, but shamans and demons, earth spirits, and fairies lived on. The eagle of the czars had not formed the country; the Soviet star had merely wrecked the churches and converted the ribbons of fields into one endless prairie. The earth remained greater and mightier than the man, who, while he might have an abode here, couldn't be said to live here. The farmer hid himself in his house, filled his lamp with oil; he had bread and toil, and he sluggishly entrusted himself to the blessing of the soil. The muzhik remained the dominant type. The land had no history. The court of the czars played political theater, landowners and nobles diverted themselves with culture, and the machines of the new era drove the unemployed into the cities, fugitives from the tractors, but it was all superficial. The age of the proletariat began, everyone occupied his own space and his own wants, but never his life, and in his soul, man remained a wanderer.

Though the proud women and upright men of the Ukraine loved the earth, and the Don Cossacks, like the Kalmucks and the Tatars, felt at home in the steppe that bore and nourished them; while the deracinated people might belong to their cities; in the division of their souls and under the spirits of the landscape they found no rest. Slaves and tyrants, murderers and saints, fools and prophets, they never became as one in their souls, and the masses lived as in a never-ending sleep. The anarchist with his pathos, the nihilist with his sarcasm, hate, and bile remained cheek by jowl with the sleepy peasant and the stooped worker. The brother of the humble worshipper became a fanatical destroyer of churches, and the primitive fatalist had the irredentist critic for a neighbor. Divided like the climate, an alternation between lurid oppositions, such were the people too.

And so I experienced the gigantic land of Russia on this voyage, often more through dreams and fleeting sights than from a predominantly literary understanding of it.

We Westerners could not understand these people or their country. Centuries sundered us from their daily reality, their spirit, and their will, and the only fruits the traveler took home with him were those that he brought out with him, already ripening. It was the boundless, the ungraspable, the overwhelming quality of this soil, this twilit land that pushed us back within our own borders and that we eyed doubtfully, and were afraid of, and could not bear, as if the daemon and the spirit of Russia preserved the land from such unsolicited, unqualified visitors. We took only riddles, clues, and doubts back home with us, and our conclusions contained neither truth nor meaning. A thousand words and pronouncements provided no valid form, and only what we experienced in war and the suffering we saw was true.

Perhaps those people were right who referred to the Russians as a coming people and thought that visitors there were witnesses to some inner maturation: to be starting over, to stand under the red dawn of a new age and grow into the future, fed at once by the millennia and by youth. We too became aware of this great preparation, introspection, and openness to destiny. But when we experienced its winter, then Russia became a *via crucis* to us, a Golgotha, and the Russian was man on an everlasting Good Friday. This we were taught by the war. But we knew that after the war, the black and yellow soils, clay and sand, loam and peat would lie there as if they had never been touched, the plain unconquered, and the people there would have remained strangers to us. The soul poured itself out into this landscape, became empty, and filled itself again with dire need. And by the end nothing would have happened.

But perhaps the land once came to meet us in peace, when we carried our sadness and our melancholy through the gloomy beauty of Ruthenia's forests, when we were lonely under the gray skies, sniffing the heartsickness of the foggy hills and thin grasses in the autumn wind, and went missing in their majesty. When we experienced the Ukrainian summer as on our so-friendly visit, loving the villages under fruit trees, and the tall poplars lending their shade to the white thatched cottages, hung with golden ears of maize; when we brushed through the fertile, flowering, ripening prodigality of the fields; when we drank in the red evenings to the singing of women and saw wild dances at their celebrations; and when we stood in the plain, merely human, naked and offered to God, who was everywhere near, threatening and vindictive, demanding and summoning, so that the persecuted man felt like fleeing into any valley and hiding in any available hollow from the ineluctable; when the grass danced before God, when the ignorant beast pastured in divine peace and the farmer did his daily work, and when the stranger succumbed to his demons or was torn to shreds by an attack from God.

This I had learned from Rilke and from the poets of Russia. We had to see the writers' models in the big cities, the song and dance of the boyars in the opera, the celebrations of Cossacks and maids in bars, to take part in the feasts of the rich, and to beg and suffer with the poor, work and live there. Maybe then we might overcome this landscape. But perhaps all we experienced then were memories of the war, drawing erroneous comparisons, and everything remained elusive and impalpable as ever for the visitor from the West.

Meanwhile the Russian soil indifferently swallowed quantities of blood and bones. The decomposing corpse nourished the insouciant tree and the corn on barren and rich soil, and the grass straightened itself again where the soldier's boot had once tramped it down. Thousands of years passed, and the Russian had only one aspect, and the only victor remained the earth.

So I dreamed the livelong summer day and still didn't believe in my pictures and the shapes they made in me. I thought on, and looked for the forces that were ruling in Russia today, trying to work for change.

Once I hadn't known much about Russia. I had thought

only of an endlessly large, unknown, unpopulated, and poverty-stricken country, with summers that burned like straw fires, endless winters in icy rigor and snow. Hunting stories from the forests of Siberia, mines in the Urals, gold diggers and adventurers, steppes and droughts and mythical cities. But beyond a few details, nothing corresponded to the actuality. The fantastic inventions of Gogol, Dostoevsky's psychology, and the names of Tolstoy, Pushkin, Chekhov, Korolenko, Andreyev, Gorky, Turgenev, Prishvin, Leskov only talked about themselves. The history books had nothing to say about the essential things. The music of Mussorgsky, Rimsky-Korsakov, Glazunov, Borodin, Rachmaninov, Stravinsky, and Tchaikovsky gave us only a dreamland and magic world, no true form. They were the lost traces of a dead time.

From the living we learned nothing. The borders were down, and we believed as little of the newspapers as we did the banned books we sometimes got ahold of. And the same with my pondering about things I had seen myself, whose sources, a planetary display, were as dreamy and insubstantial as our knowledge of them.

A vast, unimaginable effort had taken place. A century had been pressed into twenty years, plan after plan drawn up and fanatically pursued and put into effect with colossal expenditure of energy and material. It demanded huge sacrifices in terms of shortages, difficulties, material, labor, and spirit. Many things remained attempt, bold experiment. Facades were built, fragments, but sometimes it felt like nothing more than the play of a gigantic baby. But in these generations of Russians were stored energies and substances that promised completion; the hurried and botched were subjected to a process of labor that gulped them down whole. People formed themselves in accordance with the will of the time, became technicians, engineers, workers, organizers, and finally elements of the Red Army, which stood there like a mechanical colossus, a sort of robot, a titanic sum of spirit, weaponry, men, faith, and power. Total mobilization had taken place in Russia, as much as at home.

I was frightened. I no longer thought in my own language: I had learned that from Ernst Jünger. What he had seen in his figure of the worker had become fact. Relieved to be rid of my pointless thinking and desire to understand, I started to reread his work.

Kharkov. War revealed what had taken place and what had become of Russia. We saw gigantic buildings, palaces of administration and tenements side by side with tiny huts that cowered in their shade. Stations and buildings had been destroyed. We noticed nothing of the life within them. We saw figures that might have emerged from the pages of Russian authors, yet we were unable to see into their souls. We smoked makhorka and drank lemonade, but even that didn't tell us anything about the way people lived and ate and drank. We saw only the uniforms of the soldiers in battle, not the human beings, only the masses in the streets, not their purpose and life. We encountered ruins and half-suspected they might be unfinished new buildings. War multiplied our estrangement. Inferno.

We turned back into ourselves and our destinies.

We traveled to Kursk, to our adventure. Hospital trains full of wounded from the summer offensive passed us. We were headed for war, for the proximity of death, and in our exaltation, we thought of ourselves as doomed. We took on the attitude as if it were a mask. In long conversations we thought about the meaning and value of our destiny; pain and seriousness appeared on our countenances and yielded silently to the law. We were moved by dreams of Crusades, and we decorated ourselves with roses for battle and dying. The roses withered; in the end there was only death. The yearnings of youth pulled us toward the distance, we tasted the lees of our days, and still each of us hoped to be the envoy who one day would take home news of the catastrophe. We desired completion and still hoped to give destiny the slip.

Kursk. We got out and lay down in the wilderness of a garden. Plaster figures of Russian boys and girls stood by the paths. The opera was in ruins; the church was a ravaged museum of godlessness; a smaller church we found with new icons and altar. The dwellings, poor and colorless, resembled the landscape.

We went to the soldiers' home and read, played chess, and played on the pedal-less piano. Later we bought red roses from an old woman and stuck them in our buttonholes. We saw only laughing faces, heard the astonished shouts of children and women, and some girls shot us fiery glances. We dubbed ourselves the Rosenkavaliers.

From a terrace we gazed out into the dying evening and talked of death, the coming battles, and the remote prospect of returning home.

We rode on a goods train as far as Okhochevka. There we put up tents. At night, wind and rain drummed against the canvas and shook the guy ropes. We felt protected and told ghost stories.

Under gray morning skies, we awaited orders. We marched.

Rain alternated with broiling sun. Before long we felt the burden of the march. We were carrying full packs, our rifles pressed against our shoulders. Our blood grew sluggish; we were reeling and dizzy. Thirst tormented us; we found nothing to drink. We were on the road past nightfall, and then we were permitted to put up our tents in the rain and sleep. Russian planes circled overhead, German fighters and bombers buzzed past us on their way to the battle at Voronezh.

More marching. The road vanished by our efforts, and our thirst became unendurable.

A well. Brief rest. We lowered our buckets. Winching them up seemed to take forever. Then we drank, repeatedly, icy, revivifying water, washed the salt sweat off our faces, cooled our pulse points, and slumped back in the shade. We bandaged up our inflamed, sore, blistered feet. Off again.

I couldn't keep going for much longer. The quantities of water I had drunk made me shake. I felt sick. Several men collapsed. Rest. I too stayed behind. Then we traveled on a truck after the marching column and stopped in Kolbnar.

There I lay in the gutter, unable to walk, enfeebled by wild heart palpitations. My comrades carried me into a tent. The following morning I went to the doctor and was put on the sick list. I was told to go back to Kursk for observation. And so I took my leave of my comrades, the Rosenkavaliers, and became the envoy who brought the news of their dying and their readiness to die.

THE JOURNEY WEST

Away in the distance, the others were marching toward the enemy, a long, tired line of them, widely spaced, in the endlessness of Russia. A little dust enwrapped them, and the road faded into the distance. I watched them go.

A goods train came to pick up the wounded. There was barely any room for the sick, but with my new companions, I clambered up onto the roof of the first wagon. The locomotive started to pull. My journey west began.

Slowly we traveled into the evening. Dense smoke swathed us. Like coal miners with crusted black faces, we laughed at one another.

Going home!

I went very quiet. I saw the track where we had marched the day before, miserable and drained, one of the numberless roads where we had marched, whose dust still clung to our boots. Meadow scent and hay smell mixed with coal smoke. The wind cut at my face. I was transported into a limitless serenity.

We spent the night in Okhochevka. Noon the next day we were back in Kursk.

Trucks carried us to chaotic scenes at the hospital. A red multistory building took us in, a warren of untended soldiers, wounded men in old bandages, men groaning, delirious, and sapped. One of the doctors had suffered a nervous collapse, the other examined only when wholly drunk, his bottle of schnapps in among instruments and bandages, and he sent every wounded man home. To me too he gave a pass back to Warsaw.

That night the war was raging over Kursk. Russian planes bombed the city. A munitions train went up in an astonishing fireworks. Searchlights drilled into the darkness, ack-ack batteries fired, and bombs whooshed down into the night.

Goods trains shipped us to Warsaw. On the way we bought strawberries from Russian women and sat in the doorways, sleeping on benches, or on fouled straw. We didn't ask; we were long since used to it all.

Day and night the train rumbled on. Everything was adventure; nothing was danger anymore. Those condemned to die experienced mercy. In the evenings the forests stood there in infinite silence, while heaven shook out its stars.

Going home.

Warsaw. I soon felt better. I played music with a singer and a cellist and kidded around with the nurses. Only the nights were hard. I couldn't sleep for nerves, and the excitements of the trip, the doubts and hopes of the man going home, still took effect on me. Soon I wasn't supplied with morphine anymore.

So I got up again, dressed in the dark, and wandered around the quiet corridors. I ran into the night nurse, who took me back to her room. Every so often she would tour the wards, listen to the soldiers at rest, bring them medicines, and come back to me. We talked all night. I didn't tell her much. From her, though, I heard the tragedy of a woman, a nurse in wartime.

No woman, not even a whore, could have experienced men as naked and shameless as she did. Not only the helpless, bleeding, purulent body, which she tended, lay naked before her. The soul didn't hide itself either. She lived a life among wounds, pus, mutilations, pain, and excrements. The soldiers came to her, just torn away from the front, from an unwilling continence. The nurse was the first woman they had seen, often enough the only one. Another being in uniform, another form without a face, and therefore nothing but sex in disguise. The nurse saw only animals, only uniforms, with a quivering piece of meat in them, that just lately had been suffering, and, the moment it started to feel better, was desirous. She saw the eyes of the soldiers. They followed her, watched her walk, groped under her dress. One disappointment followed another. Like children, the soldiers first put themselves in the care of her hands, and their eyes implored her for a kindly word. The nurse trusted them, laughed with them, and the patient got better. His condition improved. He wasn't capable of gratitude. The nurse didn't demand it either. But now began the double entendres, the suggestions, jokes, cracks. The nurse was still able to laugh with them, to understand the crude manners, and let the human being, the soldier, behave as he felt he had to. But the soldiers didn't recognize the limits. The animal in them grew stronger. They desired any woman, and there was only the nurse. Now her comradeship was misused. She couldn't establish any respect; her humor and kindheartedness failed. Squalor had the upper hand, and the hatred at not obtaining the booty expressed itself in foul tirades.

I had seen it all for myself. But the nurse had more to say.

There were some who adapted to the men. They became whores. They didn't love them, but they helped themselves to a male from out of the uniformed mass. It was one beast among so many; the next day they chose a different one. These unknowing whores had an easy time of it.

Others treated the soldiers as naughty children, with the skepticism of mothers who are apt to resign, or nuns who do their work out of compassion and, for love of Christ, don't ask for the world or any reward, who long ago renounced, and didn't have any fear of the soldiers either. Most of the nurses, though, were young.

She stroked her hair. I didn't look at her. She spoke on, softly.

It was hardest for the women. They felt like women, they wanted to remain women, they did their work in the war, and they did it willingly. But one day they wanted to love and marry and have children with just one of these men. And now there were a thousand soldiers talking to them about love, till they stopped believing in it. In the mass the individual lost his value and identity. The nurse came to the conclusion that all men must be the same. No exception, no serious-faced patient was able to persuade her otherwise. Patients too, they had only sex in mind. The nurses no longer believed in being and in heart. If they once felt tenderness and gave themselves, then the naked animal, the soldier, would reappear, and they would hear in every word of love nothing but hidden lust, from every sigh just a harsh groan. And so they became critical and suspicious, made comparisons, and still couldn't find any safe refuge. In the end they found their own virginity ridiculous in such a world. Maybe they clung to the more impressive mask of a doctor. But when they thought of an hour of love with him, they would feel alarmed. The mask would drop, disappointment would return, still more bitter, never to be expunged.

I didn't reply to her. My soft affection for the night nurse broke as I listened to her. I didn't know if I would prove any sort of exception.

In this way whatever was dear and precious to women withered in them. Their lives lost their meaning; their loving became a swindle, or it shriveled in their fear of sex. No one, no one was spared by this war.

I traveled on to Neubrandenburg. That was my return home. I enjoyed the summer there, writing and reading. After my release I was given a period of leave. I spent it at home. I thought of my imminent departure, a third tour in the east. As long as the war went on, so long the uncertainty remained in the proximity of death. Nothing could be finished or achieved, everything remained fragmentary, and the interval made the time ahead still heavier.

All roads led into blackness.

Lithuanian Landscape

The war continued, and there was no end to the pilgrimage. I wandered back into my Russian adventure, still wearing the mask of a soldier. Every return home was a present from fate before the great danger, my abiding was only a period of grace, and the happiness and benediction of home were something like a last meal before execution. Russia would not let go of me.

I traveled toward the winter once more and to one of the focuses of the war: Rshev. I went through change after change, till I became the being that the stars wanted. Thus I experienced the hell of winter war on my contemplative journey, still playing my old masked game. I was still living more in seeming than in being. I was playing with words and roles and never became a wise man and never a monk.

God remained a stranger to me. Only in the direst emergency did I seek him out, drifting through misanthropy and contempt, and failing to learn love. Destiny once more had to conduct me to that edge, where danger, death, and pain renewed spirit, soul, and values. The beginning and ending of my pilgrimage kept returning, and when the path ended, so would my life.

Warsaw. We waited for orders to move up to the front. The days passed in idleness, and the nights belonged to our adventures among strangers in a strange land.

We strolled through the streets. Parks and mansions stood by winding lanes, tenement houses, and ruins. Department stores and plain and gold-gaudy churches were adjacent to ordinary shops, tiny bars, pubs, cafés, and junk shops. Valuable gems lay among costume jewelry and glitter. Beggars, shoeblacks, and soldiers pushed their way through the dense crowd. We passed slender, supple women, with beautiful features under their makeup, and abandoned girls. In the evenings we went to bars or nightclubs. There we experienced the excitement, the atmosphere, the charm of a metropolis. Passionate dancers stripped onstage and in sheer veils sat down among us. We drank sweet wines, listened to exciting music, saw the wealth, elegance, and peace of the clients, and found the soul of the people more easily in the eerie decadence, in play and show, under the glittery heavens of the cabaret, than in their day-to-day reality, much less their serious art. We didn't understand the songs and parodies; we felt we were homeless, deracinated wanderers, living for the moment. When we returned, girls and women offered themselves to us for a piece of bread, and our amorous adventures gave meaning to this pause before the fighting.

Lithuania. We drove through a hilly, autumnal landscape in October light. Serious, and in pensive colors, the fields lay there, pale green and brown in muted tones. Broad-leafed woods died in orgies of red and gold, and gloomy pines slowly grew into the gloomy skies. Melancholy and sorrow blew in our faces. We, though, loved the quiet beauty of this world. Life drifted simply by.

Tidy villages leaned against hills: wooden houses in plain gardens. A yellow river flowed amid gleaming streets, graveyards and ruins, copses and distant birches. The journey delighted us.

Meadows and pastures surrounded Dünaburg in the evening light. Everything drifted past us, letting itself be seen, but not touched or held. We knew this world, yet we remained guests in it; we took no part in the destinies of its people, in the breath of the earth, in the growing and withering all around us. Vitebsk, Smolensk, Vyaz'ma, and a thousand other villages and hamlets remained cameos in the endless journey.

Only the spirits of war gained in influence. Destruction and emptiness, solitude, nearness of fate, and readiness to die took us in. We no longer dreamed of necessity and barely sensed the adventure of our journey. We thought only of the madness of war, the crime of the age, and no longer shuffled the stars for our personal destinies. We lived our lives surrounded by death. No more than that.

And so we came to the front at Rshev.

The Copse at Rshev

THE TRENCH

Cool, showery days blew by with the autumn. Puddles filled with ocher-colored water and became swamps, the bottomless mire around Rshev. Leafless alders stood in the swamps; pines and birches dripped with moisture; soiled and mashed, the steppe grass lay on the ground. Murky streams flowed down soft roads. The earth was sodden. With every step, our boots sank. A shower anointed us each time we pushed aside some fir twigs. We left our tents and set off to the trenches at Tabakovo and the fairy-tale forests.

Covered with mud, coated with crusts of dirt, in sodden boots and coats, we stamped through the mire. Everything was damp and foul, the bread as much as our clothing. Rust coated our rifles. The sun alternated with night frost and snow. There was no refuge from the rainy season.

We found the trenches soft and often flooded. Water dripped into the primitive bunkers and the crude sentry holes, and the horses collapsed on the roads. A horse was more precious than a man, but we took our fate as it came, lived in our memories, and dreamed of a safe return home. Soon we became habituated to it, as though nothing had changed since the muddy season of the previous year.

Only the landscape touched us more nearly. Alder scrub, swampy hollows, and hills with vestiges of woods manifested a melancholy beauty, shifting between idyllic wasteland and frightening barrenness. We reimmersed ourselves in the mysteries of the Russian soil.

We no longer marched, no longer overnighted in villages and barns. For a long way behind the trenches, there was no house or barn intact; all that remained of Tabakovo were charred beams, bricks, gardens full of frost-spoiled vegetables, alders, and streets. Beams and boards had been stripped and used in the construction of our dugouts.

We lived in a kind of glorified rifle pit. A planked ceiling protected us against light mortar shells; a box stove afforded some warmth. We picked up firewood wherever we could. We were unable to wash, and the field kitchens in a remote ravine didn't serve us before dusk. But our serenity and calm stood us in good stead. Danger was normal, and what had once petrified us as we first set out now barely touched us. Mind and spirit accommodated the requirements of destiny.

Three hundred yards in front of us were the Russian trenches, a dip in the middle and some wire entanglements. Rifle grenades flew across without interruption, whistling and warbling over our heads or exploding on the ramparts. From time to time a light mortar would sprinkle our trench and the abutting area. Snipers made every step out of the trench a race against death. We became indifferent and didn't know whether it was resignation or trust in God.

We moved between the clay walls like funambulists, walking

on duckboards and narrow metal grids over the mud. Many of us became ill through the cold and wet. The damp clay encrusted coats and blankets; the walkways sank in the water. We were unable to change our shoes or socks. We couldn't make a fire in the daytime because the Russians would use the smoke from the wet wood to aim at. Most of the rifle pits you could get into only on your hands and knees. A tarpaulin hung in place of a door. Days were an alternation of weapons cleaning and trench work, and at night we went out on sentry duty every two or three hours, to stare into no-man's-land, in case an enemy patrol appeared, and to wait whether a bullet hit us or a direct hit from a mortar spattered our blood and brains against the trench walls. Then the guts would freeze to the clay, scraps of cloth and flesh would lie around, and someone would come across vestiges of a comrade many days later and not recognize them.

The nights brought only brief snatches of sleep. Sentry duty alternated with periods of readiness, and at dawn the risk of an attack grew. So we stood and watched, in ones and twos. Ghosts, shadows, we could hardly take in the other's face. The flares plucked us out of the darkness, dipped us into their Bengal lights for seconds at a time, suspending their harsh white, golden yellow, pale green, or bloodred fires over the motionless scene of forest edge and trench, and as they went out, they plunged us back into primal night.

Fogs lolled over the tawny yellow grass. Every shrub turned into a menacing phantom; the stalks loomed gigantically and became approaching enemies in the wind.

After midnight the waning moon climbed over the horizon, red and around over the floor of fog, as if blood were being squeezed from the hills. Gradually it swelled up like a pumpkin mask, while the night turned into a magic stage for the quiet gathering and dispersing of the silvery clouds.

Other nights shone with breadth and starry clarity. Orion and Vega, the Wain, Pisces and Gemini, and the shimmering ribbon of the Milky Way revolved calmly and endlessly around the polestar, indifferent to war and peace on this planet. Below them, luminous bursts of tracer streaked hither and thither. The beauty and lostness of the firmament were of no concern to us. Dead tired, freezing, yearning, powerless soldiers on sentry duty, we were here to kill. Machine guns hammered briefly and thinly; a shell struck: That was all that mattered in our world.

Full moon, the bright nights of the Russian north. The no-man's-land lay charmed in the white glare and sheen, and the night became a magical day. We could see across almost as far as the Russian lines. Mist rose, the cold sniffed us out, and the dream god carried us all home.

Dawn brought a sacred lull. Daybreak occurred like a relieving dream. The beauty of those hours was worth nights of fear and travail. Some of those dangers and difficulties shook and confused us. The feeling of existence strengthened through time and suffering, and an orbic enthusiasm carried us through deadly hours. In the midst of death we knew: *We are!*

The sun went down in apocalyptic colors. Every scene became precious because it was between goodbye and return home. Night passed, and like a dawn, a new, ever more miraculous return lay behind all our adventurous wanderings.

One night, going back to the dugout with food, we lost our way. We leaped over a collapsed trench into no-man's-land and ran on as far as the Russian wires. But then we found our way unmolested and looked back on our reckless undertaking as on a kind of comedy.

The night frosts grew colder, the earth froze, and sometimes we caught the scent of rime and snow in the air. Autumn was coming to an end. The second winter campaign in Russia was beginning.

We withdrew our antitank gun from the trench. We lugged it back across trenches and no-man's-land. One man was wounded; a horse died the next day. Another position, less exposed, farther away from the enemy, took us in. Life went on, but death remained our daily bread.

SNOWY WASTES

Not far from the fairy-tale wood our bunker lay in a bomb crater. Low vegetation poked bare stalks across the saps, and all around, the bleak steppe spread its expanse. We watched through the nights, digging under a sickle moon. The fireworks of flares played away in the distance, and we were glad to be dwelling in greater security. Our combativeness had long since been transmuted into a meek endurance.

We made ourselves as comfortable as we could in the limited space. The bunker was warm and offered a bench and a table and enough room to sleep. We didn't need more than that. With brandy, hot lemonade, and toast, we had ourselves the small joys of life.

The front became restless. At night there was a crashing and rattling in the trenches, there were flashes everywhere, and we grew anxious. But before long, calm returned. Days of bright sunshine followed, of an unbelievable luminosity that only the Russian winter could produce over the frozen landscape. We found frozen daisies, tiny blue stars of blossom, and withered leaves. Frost breathed over the land, and we sat by the stove. The wood crackled, the flames danced, the wind sang in the stovepipe, and outside, the stars wheeled by.

After midnight there was profound darkness. The skies were occluded by thick clouds, a strong breeze got up, and then the snow whirled over the plain, the yellow grasses and woods, lay there in white flecks and streaks, filled up the hollows, and gradually converted the land. A yellow-gray sky gaped down. With staring eyes, we looked about us. As long as we stayed awake, our souls could not die.

The winter remained mild for a long time. We were kitted out with woolens and padded suits against snow and cold. Felt boots arrived, and the soldier's life was easier to bear.

Pale sky, details of snow work on branches and grass, glittering hoarfrost in the morning light, and quiet on the front: We loved the world when it was like that.

My comrades were dispatched to Olinin, where the Russians were trying hard to make a breakthrough. They froze, were wounded, but had to hold out; they suffered from frostbite, lived in dugouts in the snow, without any stoves, and returned weeks later half starved, sick, and ghostly, a clutch of survivors from dire necessity. I stayed behind on my own, armed only with a pistol, to guard the bunker and keep order.

So, in the middle of my second winter campaign, I was living a kind of hermit's life. I chopped wood and burned it, brewed myself coffee, wrote, and sang to myself. The only time I ever saw a fellow human being was when I was getting food.

By the light of a candle or oil lamp I sat at the table, listened to the humming and crackling of the little stove, stared into the dying embers or the flickering dance of flames, dreamed, and killed time. From time to time I received visits from some other solitary, and we told each other about our lives in peacetime, our war postings and our hopes, stared out into the driving snow, and, on quiet days, walked beside the trenches, as through a miniature glacier world.

Everything that had appeared so important outside sank in my inner peace. It was only in my heart that the fullness of pictures and dreams lived on. I was living from stocks laid down in the distant past. There were no revelations but light and falling snow; flickering of fire and moonlight became events to me. I lived like a hermit all alone in space, far from the war and the noisy bustle of the world.

Dusk. I pulled on my camouflage suit, picked up my mess tin and field bottle, raised the sheet away from the entrance, and stepped outside.

A blizzard was racing over the plain; it almost took the breath away from my mouth. A dense veil of dancing, whirling, tumbling flakes enwrapped me, and the sharp wind cut into my face like a razor. Through the gray-white whirling and seething, I couldn't see the sky, and the blanket of snow deepened incessantly. Only for a few steps could I make out the ground underfoot, a tree, a shrub. I struck out in the approximate direction of the church and leaned into the howling storm. It blew over the land with the hooting and whining of a foghorn.

I had been walking for a long time, struggling on, bathed in sweat, and still hadn't reached the path to the church defile. At last I did encounter a track, but it wasn't one I knew. I had never been here before. I crossed it, and the dusk tipped blue and murky gray inks into the chasing white. I hurried, so as not to be late, and suddenly saw a wood by my side, a low stand of trees— not a forest, not the familiar fairy-tale wood. I must have slipped through a space between the trenches into no-man's-land.

I felt uncertain and turned back. The snow had wiped out my footprints, and space seemed to blur in the half-light. I no longer knew which way to turn. The foghorn boomed in my ear incessantly.

I hit the road again and this time followed it. No traces of truck or sleigh traffic marked it. I reached another piece of wood and heard the slow ticking of Russian machine guns. Then a hail of bullets clattered past me. I dropped to the ground, took the safety off my pistol. I crept back, went down the road the other way, and encountered a shot-up armored car. But there were many like that. Nearby I saw the ruins of a village, not Tabakovo, not Pondarovo. I looked in vain. I shouted into the din, ran in circles, stopped, panting, stood there exhausted, helpless, full of uncertainty and fear in the night. It had gotten dark, and the snowstorm didn't let up.

I gave up the pointless enterprise, crawled into the armored car, lit a cigarette, and decided to wait for day to break or the storm to blow over. Indifferent to the danger and dog-tired, I fell asleep.

Awakening after midnight, I stood trembling and reeling on the street. The blizzard had let up. I found a telephone line and followed it. It took me to the ravine, and from there I soon found my way back. I got to the bunker exhausted, lit a fire, ate a piece of old bread, and lay down. But I was unable to sleep for many hours. The foghorn howled in my ears, and I was glad when the day arrived.

When I awoke, I was snowed in. The early light was dimmed. A thick wall of snow had buried me. My comrades came calling and dug me out. The fairy-tale forest stood there all peacefully, the hills white; white coats draped the firs, the white bunkers and trenches, there were no tracks in the virginal snow. And yet the demons of this landscape were persecuting me, filling my soul with icy silence and a fatalism that made me hold on and endure like grass and tree. But perhaps they were doing their bit to assimilate the inner man to his fate, to enable him to suffer the inhuman.

My contemplative hermit life continued. One night the snow

creaked from cautious footsteps. I heard Russian spoken, and I clutched my pistol at the ready. But the patrol failed to spot the snowed-in entrance and went on its way.

And then I left the snowy wastes.

THE FAIRY-TALE FOREST

In the fairy-tale forest a subterranean city was coming into being. Bunker lined up by the side of bunker, all down the road. Just as into the last house on the edge of the world, I moved in with a mortar unit facing the enemy, to serve as machine gunner against shock troops and scouts.

We lived in plenty of space and warmth, were given plenty of food, put out few sentries, and were allowed enough sleep.

This was where I celebrated Advent Sunday, the time of preparation. Usually on the qui vive, I now settled in to wait for the promise to be redeemed. A presentiment of terrible events alternated with high spirits and moodiness. I acquired more confidence and calmly remembered the previous year's Advent.

The Russians assembled reinforcements opposite us. An increased stage of alert was ordered. It began to thaw. The snow melted and dribbled down the walls of the trenches, the earth softened, and meltwater soaked our boots and made the felt heavy and cold. The bare trees stared into chill gray days, and the ice cracked in the fishing pond.

Russian deserters brought news of a planned attack, and we were on the alert.

For four days and three nights we had no sleep, always in our heavy winter tunics. The stove remained lit, sweat ran down our foreheads, and in the icy draft our feet froze. The cold applied its wolf's teeth again. But the drips continued to fall from the ceiling of the bunker. Vainly we put out tarpaulins. Whatever we touched was damp and mired; our trousers and coats were clammy; our pallets were covered with clumps of mud. We waited, choked down our moldy bread, and nothing happened.

Alert. Our weapons froze. The shoes sat on our feet like a layer of ice. Alert. Equally prepared to die or flee. It mattered little whether it was a Russian bullet that brought us down or our own barrage, which would probably be leveled at our positions; whether we broke down on the road and died of exhaustion or froze to death on sentry duty in the endless nights. One hour, and we lost all sensation in our hands and feet; a second, and the body shook as in fever, trembled, shook, deadened; three hours, and the blood slowed, dreams came—and suddenly the relief brought the half-demented sentry back to ghastly life. We thawed out, stared at one another, a ghostly ring of seven deathly pale soldiers, discolored by bunker fug, smoke, and soot, with wild hair and desperate eyes, tormented by lice.

In our mess tins, remnants of food decomposed. We hid all clocks; time didn't move. Waiting became a torment. It wore us out. Everything lost meaning and purpose, and we longed for the relief of conflict. A wounded man was sent back bandaged up with paper. Men went missing. We had to hold out. We were soldiers and the pioneers of a great new age that we didn't believe in. Everything passed. Before long, night darkened over the battlefield, and the tracks of wolves multiplied in the snow. Decomposition took us in its loving caress. We dreamed of youth, before the war stole it from us, pictured our unlived lives yearningly to ourselves: There was a night that was full of drinking, singing, dancing, kissing, and there were a thousand others full of music, magic, ecstasy, laughter, dreaming, walking, and blissful sadness. But they were never ours. We saw the snow: God had made it, as he had made us. We thought of home, the books we had to burn along with their lies. We had to go home, bolt the doors, view as from a distance the decline of the West, and strangle our sons, the instant their mothers had given birth to them, so that there would be no more war in this world. Life was great, Advent, and the Savior at hand; already the Russian munitions factories were filling shells with our names on them. We added to the number of birch crosses with steel helmets dangling on them where men who had been turned into beasts rotted away. That was the accomplishment of this war.

And so we plunged into despair. Gallows humor failed us. This suffering was proof against irony, and we merely laughed in the grinning face of our misery. Fiendish grimaces flowered on the dungy bed of our Advent.

We could stand to wait in our bunker no longer. As soon as day broke, we hurried out to the edge of the fairy-tale forest. Fresh snow had fallen, and we could see down the long slope to the fishing pond.

In front of us stretched the demonic landscape of war. Fog in dense swaths lifted out of the gully and masked the coniferous heights opposite with dim haze. The plain faded away into the distance with the gray, pale reddish evening sky. Blue-white shadows and yellow lights played over the snow. There was no one in sight, no animal, no word, no birdcall. Only the bunkers, slowly emitting white smoke from their wet-wood fires, which mounted in frozen strips over the valley, as though ghostly blacksmiths were pouring the bullets for the coming battle.

Slowly we headed back into the fairy-tale forest. Snow had fallen overnight, lay thick and soft on the ground, and the branches bore its mild weight. Beautiful and silent, the wood contrasted with the foggy ground in the early light.

Abruptly the great symphony of war struck up and surged over it. We heard the detonations of the Russian artillery, bounced forward from the hills behind their lines. The shells exploded way back in our hinterland. The echo thundered, compounded itself into an elemental roar, and went on resounding like a choir of ghosts. Then the first impacts were heard in the little wood. Artillery shells burst with dull thumps; tank rounds and antitank munitions came whistling and howling and blew up with shrill crashes. Mortar shells plummeted down without notice. In between, machine guns were threading their deadly nets. The salvos of Russian smoke projectors came drumming toward us. There was an incessant shrieking, rumbling, whistling, howling, and droning that swelled into a storm and went under in an endless rolling thunder, in which we couldn't distinguish the individual discharges and explosions. This was drumfire.

We sat in the bunker fully dressed with our weapons at the ready. Two layers of beams and a few shovelfuls of earth were all that protected us, and still, it felt like a relief from the crippling stiflement of waiting. The battle was under way, and the fighting couldn't be any worse than this overture.

The bunker trembled and shook. Calmly we looked out into the fury, into fire, flying clumps of earth, and smoke. Black dust fountained up vertically and came spattering down. A rain of splinters and frozen clay came down outside the door. Gray-brown, yellowish black, and pale gray swaths of gunpowder smoke blew by. The vapor scraped our lungs and stung our eyes.

As suddenly as it had begun, the raging terror ended, passing farther into our hinterland. The telephone lines were shredded, no runners dared go out, but we knew: At this very moment the first wave of Russians would be charging against the trenches in front of us. We hurried to the mortar, rigged up the machine gun. And saw them coming: in white winter camouflage, in groups and lines. Defensive fire began. We saw them fall, falter, and flee. An hour passed.

The second wave also broke under our combined machine-gun, infantry artillery, and mortar fire. Then night started to fall. The dead lay a long way in front of us. The wounded crawled back. Our wounded were carried to the doctor. It was eerily quiet, except for the occasional shot, like a delayed echo of the noise of the day.

By now the fairy-tale forest had undergone a transformation. The snow was no longer white; rather, it was covered with a crust of powder slime, trodden underfoot, mixed with dust, shrapnel, and earth, all of which meant that the once-white forest floor gave off nothing more than an uncertain ghostly glimmer in the early evening. The wood itself seemed to have been partially cleared. Piles of uprooted trees lay about, shell crater was planted by shell crater, and the shells had sheared the frozen branches off the trunks. Shredded and broken, the damaged branches stretched out, the bark lacerated by shrapnel. The firs were bare torsos, robbed of their smashed needled twigs. The beauty and life of the wood had fallen victim to the war, just like all the dead and wounded all about.

We survivors, though, loved the danger, which we preferred to the murderous waiting around. In this battle of matériel, life proved itself to be the stronger in its orgiastic desire to *be*. The war conducted us into a dreamy place, and men who otherwise were perfectly peaceable characters felt a secret yearning for horrid feats of endurance and arms. The primal man awoke in us. Instinct replaced intellect and feeling, and a transcendent vitalism adopted us.

But now we returned to our bunker sobered, exhausted, and frozen.

That night the weapons spoke once more. There was a dialogue of machine guns, bickering from trench to trench. On sentry duty we listened. Foggy, snow-bright nights with flares burning out high up in the haze, giving us mute ghosts some human traits. Here a German machine gun called out to the enemy in rapid, dry stabs of fire that we were there, waiting and alert, and then the calmer ticking of a Russian one replied after a short interval or spoke up as our weapon fell silent. The fugal echo of the bullets was heard awhile longer.

This was a concert of technical orchestras, of mechanical instruments, played upon by their victims. Metal ruled. Grass and trees had to suffer as much as humans.

The following day heard a noisy anarchy of warring voices. Pell-mell the fire of artillery, smoke projectors, tank guns, and mortars. The last attacks faltered in front of our wire entanglements. By evening it was over.

We counted the fallen in front of our lines and picked out our dead and wounded, named names whose bearers were no longer alive. Almost unmoved, without regret, like mere statistical data, from which we passed on to the duties of the day.

One member of our platoon had received a direct hit. We picked up his limbs from the blood-crusted snow, scraped the mass of flesh and guts together, and sprinkled earth over brains and blood. What was left, almost weightless, we wrapped in canvas and buried outside Tabakovo, as if the matériel war had turned us into soulless machines.

Many times the dead could find no rest either. They lay there for weeks sometimes in summer, decomposing in cornfields while the blowflies grubbed around in their eyes, till someone found them, and a burial commando sheeted them, loaded up the slimy mass, and buried it in a war cemetery for fallen heroes. In this way, even the graves outside Tabakovo were dug up, and the remains buried elsewhere. There they rested in peace, and their deeds in everlasting renown.

Afterward we were finally allowed to sleep. A few collapsed

into almost unconscious exhaustion; the rest of us remained awake. Each time we nodded off, the shells whined into our consciousness and shook us awake, and in the silence outside, the roar of memory seemed to be amplified. We were still swaying along the bridge between life and death.

Time and time again I relived those minutes when I lay unprotected in a crater, and the drumfire flared up around, plowed the crater rim, and dumped snow and dirt on me till I blacked out. My comrades dug me up, carried me to a bunker, and thought I was dead. When I awoke, it was as though I had come from another world.

Because we were living in close proximity to death, there was nothing difficult about dying. It was the hesitancy and ubiquitousness of death that made him so great and terrible. His favorites were not those who were long spared, but those who died swiftly. Us, though, he was transforming season by season. He conducted us through the secret chambers of the soul, awoke the angel in the good man and the spirits of Cain in the bad. He filled us and peeled us, he caused us to bear fruit, and from a drop of bitter wormwood, he made a whole sea of desperation. In this way he grew over us as a victorious tree.

Like a shadow, he set himself up in front of the weak, plunged him into the laughter of despair, awoke feverish lust for life and excess, quenched the last fires of renunciation and goodness, reverence, and faith, ripped off his mask, and let him fall like rotten carrion.

Some men inclined to death like ripe fruit. The much-traveled wanderer was only too willing to drop anchor in his Hades, and the preparing for it made him happy. Death was almost like a light from within. There was no spirit world for him to wreck, and his delay crowned time.

In his nearness, all values were revised. Gold was vanity,

while every piece of bread became precious. Books shallowed or found deeper meaning; love affairs found their completion or their trickling away. Only what was essential survived. In this way death made us into new and better people.

Birch crosses told the tale of that winter.

THE GHOST WOOD

Sand slowly slipped through the hourglass, and every grain rested in God's hands. We had no sense of that.

We experienced the beginning of the New Year still in the fairy-tale forest, celebrated New Year's Eve with brandy and bold talk, and at midnight put on a fireworks display from all our weapons at once. 1943! A drunken walk followed, a sleigh ride, and we slept in late. But at the sight of the beheaded trees, the bare shrubs, that not even the hoarfrost, the visible soul of delicacy, was able to touch with life, amid all the wreckage of beauty and peace, we were regularly overcome by the feeling that all this was leading just such an unreal, spectral life as we ourselves. Then, out of nowhere, the name *ghost wood* cropped up, and before long it was everywhere.

We were like ghosts ourselves. Shelling and fighting had passed over our heads and uprooted us like the fir trees. Our masks of needles and leaves had been stripped off us by the war. Spiritually we were just as torn and disfigured as the foliage after the battle. We were incapable of thinking anything beyond: shells, detonations, explosions, black snow, blood, death. Later on, that black snow would symbolize for us the ravages the war had wrought in our young souls. Only a sheer hoarfrost veneer of toughness and danger and the fresh snow of silence concealed these wounds, till the last of us fell in the frost, piece by piece of our being broke off, and we became shadows of our former selves.

We wanted to forget the past and bury it, yet we couldn't. We started rootling about in it once more, and freighted the urns of our dreams with what we had seen.

An iron frost set in, as though a polar wind were blowing down from the stars. The white moon glowed more harshly down from the whirl of the clouds. Our hands and feet couldn't get warm. We suffered from persecution mania. Surrounded by death, we passed through these days, taking our leave. In the midst of death, we lived; we turned the commonplace on its head. We learned to hate our time and to curse the war. But within we still resisted the idea that all sacrifice was futile, so as not to fall into the despair of the soldier in an exposed, hopeless position.

The fighting was over. But it was only now that everything became real. Only now did we see how inhuman all our experience had been and try to give it some meaning and value. But reality compelled us to put away our cherished illusions. A spiritual struggle against reality began. But we found no magic word, no new illusion. Pitilessly, the war fitted into the microcosm of our world picture.

The snow lasted; the nights remained full of silence, as though everything were just a dream. If we discovered any human feeling in our hearts, God's smile seemed to blow about our brows. We started believing again in better worlds that were being born out of defeat and no-man's-land, and when we closed our eyes, images of home came toward us like a column of pilgrims, dipped in syrupy light.

One day even the dreams of soldiers would have to become lived life. We came with empty hands, but one day everything would be accomplished.

We asked questions and pondered.

We weren't living in a great time, even though many things happened in giant dimensions. Like the atoms of a storm, we passed through shocks and catastrophes and dreamed of the decline of the West as it tore itself to shreds. We participated in the tragedy; it was the triumph of the machine over man and God. The magnitude of the battles of steel and high explosives, the vast scale of undertakings, the exertions of matériel and strength in planetary space: This violence was undeniable, but it wasn't technology but spirit and intellect that made a period great.

Our own greatness was nothing but a dementia. Less than a scrap of steel, a man stood between unfettered forces, a cipher, a weapon, and an obedient body, servant to a machine. We didn't want to be like that. But we preferred to give ourselves to the chance of a battle, the mockery of a soldier's hazard, than to the certain death of law. Whether we were courageous or trembling, bold or cowardly, grimly prepared or frantic, as we went into battle, nothing weighed as anything compared with the fact that none of us went voluntarily. Only occasionally, on the brink of madness, was there the heroic sacrifice of an individual who had lost belief in his own life.

We were soldiers, dulled beings, vegetating in trenches and bunkers, wasting our time without hope, bragging, swearing, worrying, enduring, obeying: dehumanized caricatures. It was very rare for any humanity to show itself in war. And if an isolated individual wanted to write, and read and study, then there was a fight for a candle. Light was *needed* only for eating and for keeping watch but not for the mind.

Time was, war struck us as a necessity, as a divine commandment, a cosmic happening, purposing the completion and annihilation of the individual. But now we saw that war wasn't made for gods and men, that only ignorance could start an avalanche that would engulf everything. No victory, no conquest justified a single death, a man starved, frozen, lacerated, a single orphaned child. All war wanted was itself.

And so we came to understand where our willingness had gotten us, and we remembered the heroic nihilism with which we had once set out from Jaroslaw. Now we humans could survive in inhumanity and love the intoxication and beauty of destruction, praise the shards of our own destinies, adore carrion, and give it our yes. But we didn't; we had been mistaken. We were the playthings of history and probabilities.

Who were we?

Just as our winter gear ended up leaving only our eyes uncovered, so soldierliness left minimal room for the expression of human traits. We were in uniform. Not just unwashed, unshaved, lousy, and sick but also spiritually ravaged—nothing but a sum of blood, guts, and bones. Our comradeship was made from mutual dependence, from living together in next to no space. Our humor was born out of sadism, gallows humor, satire, obscenity, spite, rage, and pranks with corpses, squirted brains, lice, pus, and shit, the spiritual zero. Our stir-craziness in our bunker set little blooms of wit sprouting from the manure of need. Philosophy, ethics, and thought were replaced by self-preservation. We had no faith to sustain us, and philosophy served only to make our lot appear a little more bearable. The fact that we were soldiers was sufficient basis for criminality and degradation, for an existence in hell. Our totems were self, tobacco, food, sleep, and the whores of France.

We didn't matter. Hunger, cold, spotted fever, diphtheria and frostbite, cripples and cadavers, bombed villages, looted cities, freedom, and peace certainly didn't matter. Least of all did the individual human being matter. We could die unconcerned.

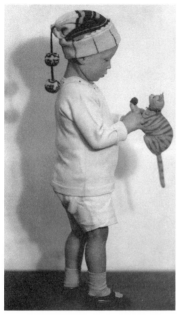

TOP LEFT: Willy Peter Reese, aged two, in 1923.

TOP RIGHT: Willy with a cousin, 1925.

LEFT: Burning the midnight oil, circa 1935.

BELOW: A student in the Mercator Secondary School, Duisberg. Willy is second from the right in the second row.

ABOVE: Testimonials from Willy's classmates in their commemorative magazine.

RIGHT: Willy as the proud high school graduate.

With his mother.

With his father.

Vacationing in Prepow on the Darss, circa 1937.

To please his father, Willy joined a bank. His traineeship came to a premature end when he was drafted in 1941.

On the exercise ground in the Eifel, June 1941. Willy is standing, fourth from the right.

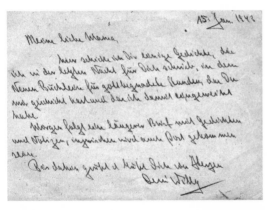

Postcard to his mother, January 15, 1943.

On a scrap of paper, Willy keeps a note of the address of a Jewish friend in Auschwitz. It reads: "Rolf N., Prisoner in protective custody, born 12/11/1920, No. 115613, Block 2a, Auschwitz Concentration Camp—Upper Silesia, Post Office 2."

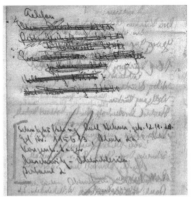

In the "Jungle of Bryansk," Russia, in summer 1943. Willy is on the far left.

Going east and west, respectively, in a drawing accompanying the letter of July 12, 1943.

Attempt at a self-portrait, July 20, 1943.

Willy with his unit, standing extreme left.

The military hospital in Oberhof, Thuringia, March 1943.

Letter to his parents, New Year's Day, 1944.

The freezing winter of 1944 in Russia.

Marching toward the Smolensk–Minsk log road.

Trying to get warm on the forest's edge at Selez.

te für die Überschwemmungszeit im Frühling zu sammeln.
Wir hungerten weiter, und unsere Därme und Mägen heil-
ten nicht. Täglich mußten mehrere Stunden Dienst im
Freien durchgeführt werden. Waffenreinigen kam hinzum,
aber für Brennholz und Verpflegung hatten wir selber
zu sorgen. Zur Post warteten wir einen Monat lang.
Die Russen griffen Dubrowka an. Sie kamen in der
Nacht. Wir leisteten keinen Widerstand mehr, denn uns
lag nichts mehr an Kampf, Opfer und dem Krieg. Wir flo-
hen nach Belaja über die Ebene, ein Rest. Panzerwagen
fuhren auf uns zu. Wir nahmen die Tarnhemden an die
Gewehre, schwenkten sie und ergaben uns. Es waren aber
deutsche Sturmgeschütze. Wir wurden gezwungen, aufzu-
steigen und fuhren nach Dubrowke zurück, nahmen es wieder, und die Russen hatten hohe Verluste. Eine andere
fliehende Gruppe war auf Befehl von der Artillerie be-
schossen werden und hatte Ausfälle.
Unsere Quartiere waren zerstört, und überall lagen
Tote umher. Über die deutschen Soldaten deckten wir eine Zeltbahn, den Kosaken zogen wir die Filzstiefel,
Mützen und auch Hosen und Unterwäsche aus und zogen sie
an. In den übrig gebliebenen Häusern rückten wir enger
zusammen. Ein Soldat hatte keine Filzstiefel mehr ge-
funden, die ausgezeichnet gegen die Kälte schützten,
und fand erst am nächsten Tag einen steifgefrorenen toten der Roten Armee. Vergeblich zerrte er an dessen
Beinen. Er nahm eine Axt und schlug dem Leichnam beide
Unterschenkel ab. Fleischsplitter flogen. Er nahm die
Stümpfe unter den Arm und stellte sie neben unser Mit-
tagessen in den Ofen. Als die Kartoffeln kochten, waren
auch die Beine aufgetaut, und er zog sich die blutigen
Filzstiefel an. Uns machte das Aas neben dem Essen so
wenig aus wie wenn einer zwischen den Mahlzeiten seine
Erfrierungen verband oder Läuse zerknackte.
Die Toten blieben liegen. Nach Wochen wurden sie mit
Schlitten zusammengefahren, gemeinsam mit Pferdekada-
vern in zerstörten Häusern aufgestapelt, mit Petroleum
übergossen und angezündet.
Sonst verging ein Tag wie der andere im müden Einer-
lei von Postenstehn, zerstückeltem Schlaf, Sorge für
Holz und Essen und dem befohlenen Dienst. Wir waren
arm geworden. Erst nach und noch trafen einzelne Decken
wieder ein und das unentbehrliche Gerät. Ich verzwei-
felte vor Heimweh und Übermüdung und bekam im bitter-
sten Frost auf Posten einen Nervenzusammenbruch, schoß

TOP LEFT: A typescript page of Willy's "war book."

TOP RIGHT: "The Beautiful She-Devil," a poem by Willy Peter Reese, April 18, 1944.

RIGHT: Red Cross Missing Persons Form from 1970: "The balance of probability is that Willy Peter Reese met his end in the course of the fighting in the Vitebsk area sometime between June 22 and 30, 1944."

+ **DEUTSCHES ROTES KREUZ**
IN DER BUNDESREPUBLIK DEUTSCHLAND
SUCHDIENST MÜNCHEN

G U T A C H T E N

Über das Schicksal des Verschollenen
Wilhelm R e e s e , geb. 22.1.21

Truppenteil: Grenadier-Regiment 279
der 95. Infanterie-Division
Vermißt seit 26. Juni 1944
DRK-Verschollenen-Bildliste Band 80, Seite 307

Ausgangspunkt für die Nachforschungen waren die dem Suchantrag
entnommenen Angaben, die in die Verschollenen-Bildliste aufge-
nommen wurden. Damit sind alle erreichbaren Heimkehrer aus Krieg
und Gefangenschaft befragt worden, von denen angenommen werden
konnte, daß sie mit dem Verschollenen zuletzt zusammengewesen
sind. Diese Befragungen fanden sowohl in der Bundesrepublik als
auch in Österreich und anderen Nachbarländern Deutschlands statt.

Ferner sind von anderen Stellen, die Unterlagen über die Verluste im 2. Weltkrieg besitzen, Informationen eingeholt worden.
In erster Linie handelt es sich hierbei um das Internationale
Komitee vom Roten Kreuz in Genf, die Deutsche Dienststelle für
die Benachrichtigung der nächsten Angehörigen von Gefallenen
der ehemaligen deutschen Wehrmacht in Berlin und die Heimatorts-
karteien.

Über diese individuellen Ermittlungen hinaus wurde die Frage
geprüft, ob der Verschollene in Gefangenschaft geraten sein
konnte. Dabei wurden die Kampfhandlungen, an denen er zuletzt
teilgenommen hat, rekonstruiert. Als Unterlage dienten dem
DRK-Suchdienst Angaben über Kameraden, die der gleichen Einheit
angehört hatten und zum selben Zeitpunkt und am selben Einsatz-
ort verschollen sind, Heimkehrerberichte, Schilderungen von
Kampfhandlungen, Kriegstagebücher sowie Heeres- und Spezialland-
karten.

Das Ergebnis aller Nachforschungen führte zu dem Schluß, daß

Wilhelm R e e s e

mit hoher Wahrscheinlichkeit bei den Kämpfen, die zwischen dem
22. und 30. Juni 1944 im Raum Witebsk geführt wurden, gefallen
ist.

THE FISHING POND

Snowstorms came. We left the ghost wood and moved into the trenches and bunkers of the fishing pond, a wide gully that a creek flowed through, swamp-sluggish, and deep in snow. Tight caverns took us in. There was no more firewood, no more candles. It was a punishment transfer.

The snowstorm foamed over hills and plains as we made our move through waist-deep snow with a sleigh, hour upon hour, panting, wheezing, cursing, and finally wearied to death. Powerless and with tears of rage, we lay in the snow, struggling to breathe. Ice crystals lashed our faces. At midnight, snow-blind and on all fours, we reached our objective.

We threw our blankets on the pallets of the unheated bunker and fell into a deathlike sleep. For one hour. Then an order sent us back out into the pitchy night. We were to clear a sap. We dug till daybreak and watched as snow kept blowing over what we had cleared. Our felt boots got wet and ripped; snow melted on our bare feet. We staggered back to our bunker as the Russians began to shoot at us, had to saw and chop wood, make fires, and then we wanted to sleep.

But we got no rest. After not many hours we had to fetch munitions and equipment, and the day declined after long miles weighed down by boxes, spades, and mortar shells. We missed the path and plunged into the creek, crawled back on firm ground, and stumbled into the bunker. We changed into boots and were sent out into the unfamiliar terrain, ran around in circles, ended up in a minefield, and fell over a trip wire. An explosion knocked us to the ground, but we remained unhurt.

Late and unsuccessful, we found our way back to our bunker and were sent from there, without food, to the main resistance line. We reached it by the light of flares, our hands gauntleted in frozen gloves, our boots frozen.

Seven hours we stood sentry, seven more hours in readiness in a bunker where there was no fire, where the snow lay a foot deep, and we shuddered with cold till we had to go out again, with frozen boots on our rigid feet, standing around on walls of snow without any cover, while a storm of ice needles, damp, flakes, and hailstones battered our faces and clothes.

That was the first night. In the morning we were given food and were allowed four hours' sleep.

A week went by. The cold came back, and the fresh snow froze over. Now we alternated at night. Some nights we stood sentry for three hours and dug for five, to keep the trenches, bunkers, and firing positions free from snow; on others we stood guard in the sap straight through, reeling, freezing, exhausted, and feverish with helpless rage.

The snowstorm came again with unexampled force. When we left the bunker that night, we could see neither ground nor sky in the blackish-gray turbulence. A gray void. We couldn't find any path and groped our way along the gully, creeping, losing our footing, and tumbling into the creek. The ice broke. The water went up past our knees, our arms were wet, and we kept on sinking. No one could hear our cries for help. Then we found firm ground, worked our way forward a step at a time, and pulled ourselves ashore. We spent another hour looking, and then we found our trench.

We borrowed dry socks and gloves and went on watch. Four lots of two hours. We stood on a high ridge of snow. The storm howled, raged, and battered at us from all directions at once, drove snow in our faces, and pushed the flakes through every chink in our battered snowsuits. We were sodden. We could barely make out the flares in the dark.

After our relief, we groped our way to the bunker, pulled off our frozen tunics, and set them down, wrapped blankets over our shoulders, and smoked with rigid fingers. No stove, knee-high snow, the wind chasing through the broken door. Our hands and feet refused to get warm. We fell asleep sitting.

Three more lots of two hours on watch, and then we went back through the still-raging storm to our own bunker. We had to spend two more hours sawing wood, light the stove with wet kindling, make coffee, and then we were given permission to sleep. Five hours, and then the next digging detail.

But when we were awakened, we were blind. The blizzard had inflamed our eyes, as though they were scratched slides. Our lids red and swollen, everything distorted, our eyes sore and teary. We had to stay awake. So we wrote letters, without seeing what we were writing. Only the thought of peace and our mothers kept us from killing ourselves. We cursed God. This exceeded what a man could take. We were desperate. There was no end in sight.

The following morning I had made up my mind. In the harsh sunlight, I crawled out of the bunker and stood up. One bullet whistled by. The second hit.

That was salvation.

Homecoming

I crawled back into the bunker and got myself bandaged up. The wound, in my right thigh, didn't bleed much and wasn't very painful. The thought that I might be saved from the hell of the fishing pond meant that I gladly took the shock and the slight stinging.

The sun was still gleaming over hoarfrost and snow. I had to wait till dusk before I could go to a doctor. Happily and, as it were, with one long sigh of relief, I sat on my pallet. My eyes grew clear again, and I wrote the glad news home and to my friends. Then I packed up my writing things, soap, towel, and books. That was all I took with me.

Propped on the shoulder of a comrade, I dragged myself to the doctor in the blue light of evening, was given a tetanus injection, and waited for a sleigh to take me to the main aid station in Sharitonovo, to the golden sounds of a Mozart symphony on the wireless.

A medical orderly took me on his arm like a child and carried me to the sleigh. The horses trotted through the clear night. Flares glimmered up, at ever increasing distances, over the forests. The snow crunched under the sleigh runners, and a meteor plunged to earth. Home! My immobile feet froze, my wound burned, but I didn't attend to pain or cold.

Going home!

In Sharitonovo the doctor cleaned out the rim of the wound and made an incision between entry and exit wound. He took off my boots and had my frozen feet massaged. The pain abated. Blood flowed through my limbs again, and blissfully I sank into a long, wonderful, and dreamless sleep.

In the morning a heated sleigh brought me to Atinovo. I was deloused and sent to a barracks, was carried into treatment on a stretcher, was supplied with brandy and cigarettes, and drank and slept through this night also.

I was awakened early, driven to Papino, and loaded onto a hospital train to Vyaz'ma. Sitting up in a passenger train, I rode west, via Smolensk and Vitebsk to Dünaburg, where, more on account of my exhausted appearance than the gravity of my wound, a kindly doctor furnished me with a pass home.

Going home!

The next evening the train pulled into Wirballen. We were taken off in pouring rain, but the rain seemed to me a consoling miracle after months in the ice and snow. I checked my small luggage and my uniform to be deloused. Nurses took off my bandages. We were bathed and sent to a waiting room to wait for our clothes and get bandaged up.

I sat in a room with two hundred naked soldiers. Soldiers with frostbite on their hands and feet, bullet wounds all over their bodies, shrapnel everywhere, swellings, and, a few, not many, with mental illnesses. Two doctors and two nurses applied bandages in this depot of human misery produced by the war. The doctors did duty for a week at a stretch, the nurses changed daily, since even the hardest hearts and the strongest nerves couldn't stand more of that pussy, rotting, bleeding chaos of pain, devastation, and screams. I saw flesh fall from dead toes and pale bones glimmer through the putrescence, ichor dribble out of festering wounds, faces disfigured by tumors, dead skin hanging in ribbons from burn wounds, and the stumps of amputated arms and legs sticking out grotesquely and spectrally from bloodless trunks.

One soldier held out the stump of his right arm to the elder of the two doctors. The surgical swabs were still in it, grown over in the course of days without medical attention. The doctor tugged at them with his pincers, and the soldier looked aside. There was dread in his eyes. He groaned and then screamed aloud like a helpless animal, a long, drawn-out, tormented, agonizing wail. The doctor's hands shook; sweat beaded on his brow. In vain he tried to come up with soothing words. Helplessly the young nurse stroked the soldier's hair and mopped the sweat on his deathly pale face. Slowly he slipped to the ground. His unconsciousness touched us all in the manner of a gift. I took refuge in a cigarette. The doctor hurriedly bandaged him up and left.

Whoever had seen this and dared to speak just one single word in favor of this war was no human; he was worse than a criminal.

It was a relief to me to breathe the cool, silent air of night as, propped on a stick, I walked to a barracks, to wait for the onward transport.

I traveled via Dresden to Oberhof Hospital, in Thuringia.

I was at home. Hills clad with evergreen forests and the last of the winter's snow, valleys with rivers swollen by meltwater, simple houses, and smooth roads outside the window of my room, which I shared with good comrades.

My wound began to hurt. The stresses of the journey had inflamed it. My leg swelled up. One evening I was lying in bed with a high temperature. I was reading a fantastic book, and its barely understood events mingled in my half sleep with memories of the white hell of the fishing pond, the ghost wood, long-forgotten adventures in the endless Russian expanses, the dead and dying, childhood dreams and celebrations, women, and the vision of Wirballen. By the time the fever broke, I was utterly exhausted.

I read, wrote, and slept.

Before long I had no peace and no way back into myself. Memories tracked me like Furies. I kept reliving the terrors of the winter campaign, hearing the howling of shells and the screams of the wounded, saw soldiers charge and fall and myself like a stranger in my destiny on the edge of no-man's-land.

I sensed the ravages the war had wrought in me, saw the overgrown gardens of my boyhood, and knew I was condemned to a shadow life in the witches' cauldron of memory. I felt abandoned by God and his angels, left out in a vast cosmos, swinging in the void between distant stars.

My pondering and self-scrutiny revolved unceasingly around the war. Carrion and horror had become my element. I was a soldier, a wicked warrior, a living corpse, a stranger among happy men, indifferent among the grieving, as incapable of happiness and grief as of pity and love. My intellectual world was sinking, and there was only death dancing on its ruins. An illusory existence among lies and masks was all that remained to me. And this was what the war had made of my life.

I remained silent.

When I was allowed to get up, I found neither peace nor oblivion, even on long walks in the wooded hills of early spring, and when I lost the ability to sleep at night, I sought refuge in wine and finally found help in morphine. It brought me only a leaden sort of sleep, and when I woke, despair, memories, and emptiness took possession of me again.

It was only from new experiences and contacts that I hoped for a cure and a turn in my fortunes.

I was released and came home.

I read, but no book offered me any signs or portents. I wrote, but words and thoughts were a colorless, formless tangle. I listened to Brahms's Requiem: For all flesh is as grass, and all the glory of man as the flower of grass. The grass is withered, and the flower fallen away. Music did nothing but multiply my grief for a lost world.

Gradually I did learn to forget and found some hope again. I traveled to Lake Constance, and there, finally, all the past sank in the fleeting happiness of a love affair. A new life, a new adventure, began, and if all these beginnings remained just an embassy from a better, kinder world, even that was something. And when it was over, I was able to say a quiet goodbye. It had to be.

Life went on.

The Russian Wandering

TRAVELING INTO SUMMER

Life went on. My return home had become a sort of flight into experience. It was only in parties, amours, travels, and events that, like an adventurer, I could find some meaning for my life, overcome the war within me, or at least hide it under a thin layer of varnish.

And so I volunteered for the front.

I wanted to fight fire with fire and war with war. I cried out for wanderings, sufferings, hardships, and the wide world, so as to slough off my introspection. To compel life by living it. I challenged my destiny to single combat. I brought with me no affirmation, no readiness, and no hope. I threw myself away, because I had lost my belief in mind and spirit and because not even love could change me or fulfill me.

In Russia I had to gather together the stray pieces of myself; there my trajectory must reach an end, either the making or the destroying of me. And so I saved for myself the last freedom that remains to the soldier, the embers in the ashes: to choose early and of my own free will the lot that I couldn't escape in any case.

No heroic nihilism, no belief in the ineluctable, and no faith in God went with me. It was purely as a wanderer and an adventure seeker that I set out this time.

I was a little crazy as I awaited the moment of departure. I drew a line under my life, wrote to thank my beloved, drank once more in the circle of my friends, spent one further night at home, and traveled along the Rhine, as if I had already caught a whiff of the great adventure.

Electrical storms were suspended over the landscape. The journey began. I left behind the bombed cities of home, the wreckage of my youth, and I stood to for the command of the hour. We celebrated the departure with wine and champagne, and at midnight I was traveling drunkenly through the unlit shapes of my hometown, buildings enjoying no more than a shadowy existence, sacrificed to the war, ruins of past felicity.

I wanted to embrace my destiny and my ruin. Secretly I was hoping for a further return home, because I did want to live out my youth and my yearning, but I agreed to die if that was what the stars had in mind for me.

Slowly the train rumbled eastward. Lódź, Warsaw, Orsha, Smolensk. I drank day and night: brandy, vodka, gin. I was barely ever sober for more than an hour at a time because then misery gripped me, dread of what lay ahead took hold of me, and the war reclaimed me. My thoughts strayed over vast areas, and contradictions multiplied. I no longer had any perspective on things.

The war had become a divinely ordained purgatory. The only thing that still had any meaning was the quest for God. Everywhere I caught already the putrid smell of irony, and it was only where the edges of things became unclear that the mysteries began. But myself I could not understand. The war had become an insane variant of introspection. I was partly responsible for it, even if I hadn't asked for terror and fear of death. But I was on my way with my fellow penitents, and my life became a sort of legend to myself. In my heart, though, the world no longer made sense, and it was only in drink that the conflicting spirits got along.

So I viewed my departure as a comedy, a chaos of contradictions and errors, masquerades of words and pictures, and suddenly the whiff of adventure overcame me again, a divine frivolity that rejected any and all responsibility. I calculated there would be enough time afterward for tears.

Once more the vast expanse of Russia lay outside the windows. Gray skies, meadows, scattered trees, rarely a building. It was raining. Hay and grain were rotting away. I slept and drank.

In the sunset at Smolensk, I heard women singing. They sang between trains that crossed here, east and west, melancholy, lost in their eerie, cruel, fertile country and a soil that would not honor any amount of sacrifice.

In the moonlit night, horns sounded. There were calls from obscure distances, coming nearer and losing themselves in other distances, a sound full of yearning, fatigue, and homesickness, and yet a romantic greeting, an embassy from life in the enemy land.

In the evening we were taken off the train at Yarzevo. We overnighted in a barn and the next day rested at Filipovo. There, after a long time on the road, I saw girls dancing in the evening again. To the monotonous sound of balalaika music, they stepped and twirled in a ring of young men, sometimes sang in soft plaint, and spun again in a mute dance, took hands with slow movements, parted them again, and exited the ring with a light bow. Their white headscarfs glowed in the sunset and went on gleaming in the rising moon; distance was reflected on their impassive faces. Crickets chirped in the mournful balalaika noise, and we soldiers sang and laughed with strangers, as if the distant sound of the front were not echoing in the ancient dance.

I was happy. In the middle of Russia, I at last felt at home. This was where I belonged; nowhere other than in this world with its horrors and sparse joys was it good to be. Only here did my soul find its strange element.

A thunderstorm was hissing, and pale yellow light crashed through the clouds. A rainbow built its laborious arch over alders, pastureland, and forest clearings. I went into position in Vorotinovo, a village where only ruins were left protruding through the tall grass and profusion of flowers. That was the critical point in our position at Vopez. The Russians were just in front of our trenches, and day and night we traded mortar shells and bombs with them.

A wild blooming and sprouting covered our trenches, and the bunker itself disappeared under a pelt of corn and weeds. In spite of that, it felt almost like a skyscraper, the way it loomed out of its slope, and not a few shells whistled hard over our heads and stuck in its upper walls.

I had no need to get acclimatized here. This was my house. I wasn't just a guest.

Nights we spent digging in the misty landscape, under the moon and stars, till blue-gray dusk. Flares whizzed past, explosive shells hit, sudden assaults of mortars forced us under cover, but the danger didn't frighten us. It soothed me to be remote from everything intellectual and from all the movements of my spirit. Letters helped against the isolation.

The muted beauty of the scenery around Vopez was now my life. Not the war. Sunrise, the movements of the clouds, dusk, and starry nights built a world where I felt cheerfully at home. Nothing but a wanderer, an adventurer, an itinerant student of life, I stared into the nameless face of war. All the powers might be striving for one another's extermination; what manned the trenches barely deserved the name of man; they were more like soulless tools of destruction, fanatics of doom. There was hardly a pause between engagements for the individual man to think of his being made in God's image and the foes to feel their shared fate. Being made a prisoner was a terror, and being wounded in no-man's-land meant almost certain death. The operation of these elemental forces provided the setting for me to live and be in magic horror, a wanderer between dust and stars in that unhinged time. Death and killing were the only aim of this tussle; there was no conflict of politics or philosophy; each man was fighting for his life and no longer for ideals and a delusory meaning; everything finally devolved to a futile waste of men and matériel.

We stayed there a few more days, bronzed by the July sun. Then orders came that we were to be relieved, and we departed at night. And so began my Russian wanderings. The uncertain tracks of that year began.

THE BATTLE

We moved out at midnight. Stars shone over no-man's-land; a cool breath came off the dewy meadows; mists shrouded the woods. We strode calmly into the beginning day, headed toward adventure, carried by our condition of strange readiness and a newly alerted courage. Pallid morning light lifted the contours from their slumbers, green and reddish lights shimmered at the edge of the clouds, and profound silence lay over the roads and the men, marching in loose file.

The sun burned. We slept in a sparse meadow. Scorched

brown earth in ascending plateaus stretched out at our feet, thin brush and wizened grass, and on the horizon a sense of hills and hazy woods. I sensed the onset of a new phase of life, bitter and cruel. But my optimism transcended the future. Never had death been so plainly present.

We marched into the tenebrous night. The noonday sun had dried the sweat on our brows, and now we were shivering and exhausted and footsore under a light dusting of rain. Thunderheads clashed over the tarmacked road. The torches of lightning lit up the shadowy land, and flares showed the front to the side of us. In Vyzhegor we rested. The rain stopped, and we marched on. We slept for a few hours of the dull gray morning in a yurt, and then we were marching again, along sandy tracks and red stone roads, sometimes reeling with exhaustion, toward Yarzevo. Rain showers alternated with piercing sun as now water, now sweat drenched us. No one thought of any marching order. Everyone just walked for himself and carried his rifle in the way he wanted to. The impression of torn boots and dirty uniforms was supplemented by sticks that we broke out of the hedges, and we rolled up our sleeves and tucked our forage caps into our belts. The sun bleached my hair and tanned our faces, which were hard and drawn with sweat and exertion.

In Yarzevo we were put on trucks. Vehicles and guns were hurriedly made fast to flatbeds, and thirteen of us were put on a goods wagon.

The July sun scorched through the roof. Heat, the smells of the sweating horses, and their piss and shit produced an intolerable atmosphere. We opened both doors, but the air remained close, and the piercing ammoniac smell sat in our lungs like a lead lining. We all suffered from heart palpitations and headaches, and a few vomited.

At night we froze in the draft that blew across the floor. All day I sat in the doorway, breathing the rushing air, which, though thick with dust, humidity, and heat, remained a blessing compared with the pestilential stink within. Villages and hills, endless cornfields, and the swampy forests of Bryansk flew by me. The corn was ripening; some shocks stood in straight rows. Damp, mold, and resin blew in from the forests. Dust clouds danced on distant roads, and many streams had run dry.

I felt strangely close to the earth. Like its trees and flowers, I felt my life blooming in this intoxicating summer; like the grass and corn, it would soon sink back into harvest and decay. Mold and rot pierced the rising of the sap; the carrion of rotten boughs sustained the young growth, just as my corpse would one day sustain the seed. A feeling of security came over me. Life was large; there was no danger. It wasn't a question of the individual shrub or stalk. The weed flowered and suffered patiently in the circle of the seasons, and sleep and death would be followed by the new birth of the spring. I didn't need to worry; dying was easy. I was a soldier, a wanderer and adventurer in no-man's-land; spiritually I was free, and free in the face of death, no more lost to life than the blossom, fruit, and seed of the rowan tree.

We were set down in Berezovka.

A baking heat scorched the land. Thirst tormented us along the march. The water in the streams and ponds was lukewarm and barely cooled our pulses. We drank it anyway, and no one fell ill.

We strode through gold-gleaming country. In the villages we saw women and girls in colorful costumes, with headscarfs and skirts in fiery red, red stitching on the white bodices over their heavy breasts, wide hips in an animal gait. In their carved, almost slitty-eyed faces, the cheekbones were prominent. Black ribbons of hair fell across low foreheads. We met few men, mostly oldsters in picturesque rags. White beards, white hair framed their weathered features.

We exchanged bread and salt for milk, which we drank as avidly as fever patients, paused briefly in exhaustion, and washed the sweat off us with well water.

In the next villages we found houses wrecked by shells, cratered roads, saw far-off clouds of smoke, and heard the distant confused hubbub of a battle. From the direction of Orel.

Alarmed old women and children peered out of their windows and shrieked when they saw our guns. They were afraid we were bringing the war back to their huts. With handfuls of salt, we bought their friendship and their trust. They told us about the sudden appearance of the Red Army and the German counterthrust and watched us go with frightened eyes. We moved on.

Ravaged gardens, trampled fields lay beside our road. A forest took us in, and we were grateful for its thin shade, cooling damp under oaks and beeches, and the broken light in a clump of pines. We rested; I went looking for raspberries in the underbrush, found a type of moss I'd never seen by the seaside, stuck flowers in my forage cap and in the muzzle of my rifle.

Ahead of us, in the blue-tinged forest, were the Russians.

We marched along the country road, through meadows and swampy dells, where the occasional shell had landed. In a little hamlet between hedges and battered trees, the inhabitants were building a bunker next to their shot-up houses. I stopped to talk to a beautiful girl. In broken German, she told me how her siblings had died in the previous days' fighting. I kissed her and hurried to catch up to my comrades.

The sun slipped down, and at twilight we reached a large village, clustered around a crumbling church. Long rows of cottages ran down from the hill into swampy valleys. Streams ran through the pastures. This was Mileyevo, our destination, the point at which the Russian breakthrough had been held. We were to occupy the neighboring villages, make communication to north and south, and hold a new line.

Dog-tired, we slept, with only a few sentries watching, and didn't know that it was only that selfsame night that the Russians had withdrawn, no farther than the other end of the village.

In the morning the battle started.

Our troops advanced toward Panov, a village to the east of Mileyevo. Early in the morning the fighting began without any sort of preliminary bombardment. We were held in reserve, to secure the flank and follow with our antitank guns.

Sporadic Russian artillery fire strafed the village and the front area. We waited behind the cover of some houses, in light rain. I played with a kitten and listened to the far-off rifle fire and the bursts of machine-gun fire, till the order came to advance.

So as not to expose the horses to danger, a column of us dragged the guns, hung with four crates of explosive shells, into position. Unobserved, we reached a hollow and traversed a creek. The water ran into our holey boots. Uphill. Our hands and arms were getting tired on the grips.

Halfway up, intense shelling began and drove us off the path. We looked for cover in the furrows of a cornfield. There we lay behind the guns and smoked and listened to the nearby falling and bursting of the shells. I studied the filigree work of nature on the whiskers and kernels of an ear of wheat and blinked in the sun.

Finally we dragged the guns farther away from the path, to avoid the shelling, and found room to make further progress on an adjacent hill. Undisturbed, we reached our provisional goal. White flares flew up out of the woods. Our troops there seemed to have been making rapid progress.

Now dense crowds of men spilled out of the forest. Our task seemed to have been done. Suddenly they spotted us and opened up on us with rapid, confused rifle fire. Only now did we make out the fleeing remnants of our attackers.

Withdrawal. We dragged the guns down the hill on the double and wound up in a swamp. Then we dragged one cannon after another through it and up the steep facing slope. The wheels sank in past the axles, while we were up to our knees in morass and water.

Leaving ourselves only a short pause for breath, then supported by stragglers, we pulled the guns farther up the hill. We were back in sight and range of the Russians, who were only a quarter of a mile behind us and closing rapidly.

Our retreat turned into a flight. We fell ever farther behind with our loads. Desperately we launched a few explosive shells into the enemy ranks. Not much effect. We ditched the rest of the ammunition and panted on to Mileyevo.

Our arms were exhausted, our knees buckled, but there was no rest, no stopping to catch our breath. Machine-gun bullets sprayed around us, smacked into the field, ripped open the ground at our feet. The first of us was felled, hit by a bullet in the heel. He crawled on, his face contorted with pain and dread. A second was hit in the head, a step away from me. We climbed over his body and didn't look back. Another man collapsed, screamed, clutched his hip, staggered up, crawled on awhile, and lay there. The fourth took a bullet in the chest. He gurgled for a while and stopped moving. Events moved past me as in a dream, mindlessly taken down. They had as little weight for me as the rain of bullets that now tore my tunic and one boot, as the nearing Russians, as all of life. With the last of our strength, we held on to the transom, while the blood pounded in our temples and our hearts raced. We knew no fear. We just pulled cannons.

Then the horses raced up with the limbers, and we fixed the guns on them, threw ourselves on the beams and barrel, and raced into the village at a crazy gallop.

There the two of us who had survived set up the gun and collapsed, dead tired, into the grass. Our lungs throbbed; the sweat dried to salty crusts on our twisted features; the last of our strength drained out of our arms and legs. Now dread flickered in our eyes. The images of the last few hours flared up briefly and submerged in our memories. We said the names of those who had died. I was staggering between dream and waking, saw everything through a veil yet somehow with excessive clarity, as if I were unconscious and also overly aware.

At that point no enthusiasm, no foaming sense of life carried me along; everything was quenched: will and fear, mind and soul. All that remained was a mechanically adaptable being that recorded events like a camera and was also at the end of its tether.

The night began with a cloudburst. We cowered under canvas, but the water got through and drenched our tunics, even as the last of the sweat was drying in our undergarments. We froze and trembled, smoked with fingers numb with tiredness and misery in the July night. We wanted to stand guard together, but toward midnight we both dropped off, sitting on the transom, till the light of morning woke us. We failed to register the danger. It wasn't giddiness. Perhaps it was the adventurer's trust in the stars. Faith in God or fatalism, submission or stubbornness, in our exhaustion apathy knew no limits.

In gray, windy morning cool, a violent bombardment of artillery, mortars, and antitank weapons set in against our rifle pits and half-fortified positions. The Russian assault commenced.

In broad waves and loose bands, the Russians emerged from their positions on the edge of the forest, a little over nine hundred yards in front of us, and advanced uprightly along the wide slope. Either side of the road there was tall, overripe corn; only in the hollow did pastureland recommence.

Defensive fire from infantry cannons punched the first holes in their ranks, but our artillery had no ammunition. Our explosive shells smashed into the enemy ranks, machine guns beefed up the barrage, but the Russians pressed forward, apparently oblivious to their losses.

The first of our wounded were ferried back. The dead were piling up in front of us, and the two of us remained by the gun. In front of us the attackers were bleeding to death, but to the side of us the last of the infantry who had been pulverized the day before were also dying. There the Russians succeeded in pushing deep into Mileyevo.

Toward noon the last of the enemy withdrew from the cornfield in front of us. We sent a few isolated shells after them. But either side of us, the battle was raging. The communication was broken; we were on our own.

We wiped the sweat from our gunpowder-blackened faces, had the sensation of dipping our hands in clay and dirt, listened to the sound of battle that was slowly drifting eastward. A runner turned up. There too, apparently, our reserves had succeeded in repulsing the Russians and holding the line.

We stared at each other. Our uniforms had both been holed again, but we were intact.

I burst out into wild sobbing. For a long time tears ran down my cheeks, washing white streaks in the layers of grime and soot. I vainly had recourse to cigarettes to calm myself, but it was an hour before I recovered.

It wasn't the nearness of death, or the intense experience of danger, or the dreadfulness of the fighting. It was relief that caused me to break down, the fleeting awareness of the appalling things I had experienced and that took the soul out of the mechanical action, so that it resumed its own uncertain being once more.

Several heavy antitank guns now began to bombard our position with large-caliber shells. I lay in my hurriedly dug rifle pit and, in spite of the proximity of the crashing shells, soon fell asleep. I was awoken by an intensification of the firing and a hail of splinters. I saw the Russians emerging from the edge of the forest and ran to my gun. On the way I was engulfed by a shower of earth from my hole, which had just taken a direct hit. A second between life and death.

We lay behind the gun, not daring to get up and shoot, as the enemy fire was getting denser all the time and machine guns also pinned us down. Our foolishness in remaining in a position familiar to the enemy became our doom.

The Russians rapidly approached. Now it hardly mattered whether we lay there and were overrun and cut to pieces or if we died in a desperate attempt at self-defense. We opened fire.

There were not many still standing when the bluish-white clouds of powder from the shells drifted away. Our detonations crashed into the general noise; there was still the shrilling of incoming ordnance. A splinter scratched my hand. I let the blood flow and went on mechanically reloading. The few riflemen in front of us were either wounded or dead. The last of the machine guns fell silent, and twenty yards to the side of us the attackers emerged from the tall corn. There had been a gun of ours standing there; maybe all the defenders were dead.

I picked up my rifle. My comrade yanked the striker out of the lock, without looking up, and stuck it in his pocket. We fired off the last bullets and fled.

A blow in the back felled me. I picked myself up, felt the blood trickling down my hip, threw away my rifle and belt, and hurried on.

When I found myself among the few survivors, I stopped. We were the last; we had already been given up. I pulled my tunic away and jerked the splinter out. An adhesive plaster would have to do by way of bandage. I took a dead man's rifle and shoved ammunition in my pockets.

We went over into counterattack, thirty men against an unknown number of enemy. Light artillery was wheeled up and turned to the side, where the Russians had penetrated even farther.

We walked upright through the gardens, past dead and wounded, Germans and Russians. Blood dried on the corn.

The sun plunged into night. Most of our little platoon had fallen. We got back to our gun and, seconds later, began firing. The last of the Russians fled past us.

The battle was over.

We watched among bodies. Hour by hour. My wound hurt, but I was alive. The Russians didn't know how few of us there were when we risked our desperate counter, how few now returned dead tired to their holes, to lie and stare into the dark. The two of us stayed alone in our position.

Reserves came. We were able to withdraw our gun to a reserve position. So doing, we passed the dead who had been brought together, fantastically illuminated by the light from a burning house and the torches of the flares.

Reddish-brown bloodstains encrusted our uniforms. Black-red gouts of blood clung to shattered faces, hung on wild hair, and punctured steel helmets. Clenched fists reached out point-lessly, casting menacing shadows. Detached limbs were laid alongside drained bodies. A solitary head grinned by a fence; two whose injuries were concealed by the dark faced each other in a spectral confrontation. In the sheen of the flames, dead eyes acquired a wild and mysterious life. A laughter produced by light and shade twitched around silent mouths, frozen in their death cries or a sardonic leer; a desperate stubbornness flickered about pressed lips. Other heads were no more than a mess of bone, blood, brain. Guts spilled out of ripped-open bellies.

Silent soldiers stood around the motionless assembly. We folded our hands.

The following day they were buried, and by the time the birch crosses were fixed over the mounds, no one knew anymore if the name fitted the carrion beneath, where heat and worms were already getting to work and that would soon put forth moss and grass. The Russian soil was quick to accept corpses of any description—those of her sons, as much as those of others.

But I was alive, and I had no fear of death as such. If I fell to-morrow, life would go on without me and my happiness or sorrow. I didn't need to worry about that. Thousands more were ready to work and to bring the task to completion, to quarrel with destiny and prevail or, like me, fall by the wayside. I didn't matter, and as for whether I was given a grave or not, I wouldn't feel it in any case.

At about midnight we moved farther back from the line, into the defile of a creek. We camouflaged our gun and finally slept for several hours.

We awoke among dead Russians. The dead were all over the place, lying in the grass, on the path, in the stream: young, strong men, with their weapons at their sides. They were the fallen of the day before; they were no longer our enemies, but still we were angry with them for soiling our drinking water. The sultry, thundery air favored their decomposition. But we did at least wash and, after two days, eat, after a long time in which we had felt no hunger. I looked at myself in a mirror and got a fright. My brow was furrowed by three deep creases, sharp lines led down either side of my nose, and my mouth was white, all blood pressed out of it. I had seen and experienced death. Perhaps I would be marked by it as long as I lived.

Stench and humidity lay over the defile. In the early dark I set off on a scouting mission, to explore the front and the condition of the land before us. I walked along a deserted village street. A dog followed me; a house cat wailed. Other than them, the place had died, its inhabitants fled. In some stalls I found starved animals. Weeds rampaged over the gardens; ripe vegetables were rotting away.

I climbed through fences and what remained of shot-up huts. Walked on through rye and potato tops, my rifle at the ready. Evening dew was brushed onto my boots and cooled my hands. I never wore a steel helmet, and I'd covered my forage cap with cornflowers and ears of grain, at once ornament and camouflage.

I wandered on into deeper darkness. The stars burned above me. No flares showed me where I was. I was deep into no-man's-land before a light went up, and I was shocked. An icy shudder gripped me. Three Russians were lying only a few steps in front of me. I jerked my rifle up to my shoulder. They didn't budge. A breeze. Cadaver smell.

As though pursued by ghosts, I turned back, still unable to find any of our men, and was relieved to see the outlines of the village street in front of me again. I smoked a cigarette inside one of the houses. My comrades were calling me, and I joined up with them again.

We brought the gun up a gentle slope and set it up in front of a garden. In the night I stood sentry and listened to cannon thunder from north and south. In front of us all was quiet. Stars slid across the black sky, the Milky Way blinked, and after midnight the waning moon rose up out of cloudscape and gloom. Trees and shrubs stood there like ghosts in its sparse light. Grass smell wafted in the cool. No whiff of carrion in the air. No footfall, no voices. I kept still and watched, and nothing happened.

The relief came. Then, like the corn and the shrubs and the dead, I slept.

Early we moved into position by the red church in Mileyevo. The battle was raging in front of us. Russian artillery shot the church into a rubble of bricks, mortar, and dust. Splinters flew around, the air pressure punched our lungs, but we remained unhurt. The fighting went on for four days, tank attacks failed, and dive-bombers attacked the Russian positions. Then there was quiet. The front settled down, and our positions were strengthened by the remaining artillery pieces.

We were moved to the southern entrance of Mileyevo. Close to the creek we found a good, clean house in a flourishing garden, and we made ourselves at home. In front of us a meadow with a few alders and poplars extended into the forest. We had no neighbors and only a few pillboxes between ourselves and the enemy.

We, though, after the days of fighting, led a cheery and blithe life, roasted chickens and slaughtered a cow, fried potatoes and mixed cucumber salad, ate fresh carrots, and played cards. After a brief shower, tropical heat began, and we spent the days lying naked in the creek. At night we were tormented by turnip fleas and bedbugs. Sleepless with the heat and the itching bites, we rolled around on our pallets and ended up sleeping in the open, till we woke up shivering in the dew and morning mist, with mosquitoes buzzing around us. We smeared flies on our bread and could barely defend ourselves.

A storm softened the leaden atmosphere. Thick fog hid the landscape in the evening and didn't leave till it got dark. We kept watch, while bullets whistled around us and smacked into the loose soil.

During those nights I felt a tingle of peril and adventure, like a form of electricity, an intensification of life that it takes war to provide. For even the wildest party or the boldest achievement in peacetime lacked the glamour of danger and the charm of proximity to death. My friend Hein had become close and dear to me; he was like fertile soil from which I grew. He worked with me and shaped me, like soft wax. He gave meaning, order, and purpose to things; he firmed up what was real, and scattered lies and illusions like chaff, and didn't alarm me. I didn't run from him, yet I loved my life as deeply and passionately as never before.

When the evening sky grew dark, the horizon continued to glimmer from the many fires. Village after village was sinking into rubble and ash. The people were driven west, their animals led away or slaughtered, the harvest torched. An insatiable work of destruction was readying the land for our departure. Roads and tracks around Mileyevo were mined, bridges and houses booby-trapped. We waited for orders to leave.

The nights poured with rain. Then a powerful sun came rampaging through the fog. Our last day in Mileyevo. I dreamed of summers by the sea and finally took my leave of my girl. My destiny was enough to fill a life, and my vague yearnings vanished under presentiments of the adventures ahead.

I was ready.

Wandering into Fall
(1943)

Departure. We strode silently off into the night, only the creaking of the carts on the sandy tracks and the whinnying of the horses joining the chirruping of the crickets. Fog ambled over fields and meadows, stars flashed up in the flimsy clouds, and the full moon doused houses, bushes, and trees in its milky gleam. The firelight of distant villages glimmered on the horizon and was reflected in the clouds. The retreat began.

We marched. Far behind us we could hear the crash of the bridges being dynamited. Mileyevo went up in flames. Barren no-man's-land was left behind. We reached the tarmac road, collected ourselves, and got into defensive formation. We, with our easily maneuverable guns, made up the rear guard. We hurried westward through fresh, dewy pastures, following the line of fires, shivering in the night wind and tired. Before long the rapid march had us mopping our brows.

We crossed the ruins of a village. Kvastovitchi. Deserted

streets, charred beams lying in the roadway. A dog howled at the moon. Stoves gaped from the ashes, and abandoned horses roved through the darkness like ghosts.

In the midst of smoke and dying fires, we were fed. Dull orange daubed the smashed stoves, collapsed walls, and scorched vegetation. A smell of burning filled the air, and a fine rain of ashes descended on us.

We moved off. Our eyes were falling shut, and we gripped hold of the cart, leaned against the guns. We were going uphill.

We made a stop at the edge of an orchard. We parked the guns under ancient beeches. We were not permitted to sleep. To the east of us Mileyevo was ablaze; to the north, the dark, forbidding forests. In front of us we could make out the outlines of the ravaged village against deeper darkness, struts, chimneys, fences, among the smoldering wood. Death and destruction marked our path, our flight.

We stood together, shivering in our coats, now struggling to stay awake and now, with that strange alertness that comes out of extreme tiredness, talking in impassioned tones of indifferent subjects. We sang the wild, senseless songs of the period, songs of drink, adventures, and whores, and finally we started dancing clumsily, like bears, grotesque dream shapes in the Russian night. We were leading a ghost life, refugees dispersed across the immense land, and as we danced in Kvastovitchi, madness flickered around our foreheads, a dance on the ruins of the village as on the ruins of our lives, dazzled by flames, swaying in the wind like hanged corpses.

Sluggish morning light seeped across the east. We found haystacks, spread out blankets, and slept till the sun rose and dangled over the devastation.

With hot, fevered faces, with hurting limbs and swollen feet, we staggered on and were given a position to hold in a cornfield, facing the end of the village. There we lay down in the sparse shade of haystacks, tormented by heat and exhaustion, stung to bits by turnip fleas, feeling infinitely empty inside, and playing cards like sluggish, lifeless machines. We were degenerate, lousy, dirty, unprincipled, indifferent. We had long since lost all interest in life and the world.

The Russians crossed Mileyevo and followed us along the tarmac road in long columns. We pulled back through deep sand into a defensive position. We went around barricades and minefields. The last abandoned houses of the village stood in ruinous gardens, themselves ruins.

At the edge of the wood that had given us a little quiet and shade on the march out of Mileyevo, into the catastrophe, we found waiting soldiers, sleeping beside their weapons, as though felled. We followed the road farther into the wood. Leaves and mold fermented in the midday heat. We disobeyed orders and rested. Overripe blueberries quenched our thirst.

We came to the north flank, a line against unknown territory. The communication was broken; our unit was all on its own. In the early evening we reached the edge of the forest. A chain of wooded hills surrounded us on all sides. We didn't know where we should point our guns.

Apathetically we threw ourselves down on the grass and slept, until we were woken by cold and damp. The earth quickly gave up the fire of the day. We shivered, covered ourselves up in hay and twigs, and went back to sleep. Once woken up, we huddled closer together, smoked, and stared at the round moon.

Finally we heard some muffled voices, the clink of weapons, and the clatter of vehicles, and we were back with the rear guard. In thick fog our spectral column slid over endless pastures, and we followed the tarmac road in an accelerated march. The morning dispelled the fog. We reached the remnants of a village, left our guns in a ditch, and slept till we were woken, this time by hunger. It was evening. The wide plain was deathly still, and the evening star shone over the hills. A red flare went up steeply into the brighter air, shattered into a shower of stars, and went out. The Russians were attacking Buyanovichi.

In an endless chain, we saw their black shapes approaching over the hills, slowly growing larger on the horizon. Shells screamed over our heads, detonating behind us with a crash. We saw their impacts, gray-black, whitish, yellow-brown clouds of gunpowder smoke, earth and dust, heard the crash, mingled with the hammering of machine guns. We did no shooting ourselves. Artillery and infantry shells smashed the waves of attackers, dispersed the survivors, and a Russian radio announcer gave orders to withdraw. This battle struck us as being like an eerie theatrical, and we didn't understand it.

An order came for a speedy departure. Contact with the enemy broke off. We remained behind in the village as a rear guard. Angry and despairing, we left our guns limbered up and slept in the gutters. Not till early the next day did we move off, on the double, as in a frantic flight. Even so, the Russians were catching up. We fled with our horses, but the other guns—rendered unserviceable—were left to fall into enemy hands.

We were marching west. We didn't know where we were going, and we didn't care. But the marching was demanding. So many sleepless nights took effect, hung like lead on our limbs: Our brows were fevered; our brains flickered with dazzlement and exhaustion. Now a heavy, unabating rain set in. The roads turned to swamp; tarpaulins and coats gave no protection against so much water. We slithered, staggered, fell, picked ourselves up, and hurried on. The Russians were coming rapidly after us, and we were still wandering around in no-man's-land. At about noon we came to a village. Dubrova.

The field kitchen was waiting for us with hot food, but it had turned rancid and inedible. The sun cut through the melting layer of clouds. Roads and meadows quickly dried, and we put up the gun in a stubble field, between corn stooks, and waited for it to get dark.

Ahead of us the hills stretched away in the brown-gray light. A few isolated shells exploded. The advanced posts withdrew, small as dwarfs in the implacable land. But the Russians did not press on.

The dusk drew dim veils over hills, dales, and clumps of alder. The temperature fell. Behind us Dubrova flickered in a series of rapidly spreading fires, like gold against the night sky. We strode behind the cart in the starless night.

We were tormented by thirst. For days we had drunk hardly anything. But now, as we peered down into the wells, all ready to dip the buckets, we saw a scummy mass, with rotten wood and thorn-apple bushes afloat on it. Other wells had been blown up, and the last blocked off by mines. Tears of rage and misery came to our eyes. What had been devised as a means of slowing the Russian advance had become a needless torture for us.

We passed through smoke and flames. Beams crashed down from burning houses; sparks whirled up in the air; timber fires smoldered on the roadway. A rain of ashes and hot dust hailed down on us, coated our faces with a layer of gray, made our eyes water. Burning air blew at us and seared our lungs. Our throats contracted. Harsh flames dazzled us. Suddenly planes roared overhead and dropped their bombs on our slow-marching columns. The cries of the wounded resounded into the bursting and whooshing of the flames. Horses broke loose and raced into the flames. Slowly we regrouped.

I collected up field bottles and mess tins and hurried off ahead to look for water. An unknown soldier joined me. At the entrance to the village we discovered an undamaged well. We clambered over ruined walls, ashes, charred beams. I tumbled into a cellar, and my companion plunged on toward the well. A deafening detonation rang out. The air pressure sent me flying onto a pile of hot ashes. Earth and pieces of wood crashed down on top of me. I leaped up. The well was gone. I never saw the soldier again.

A platoon from the rear guard suffered the same fate, and only one of them survived.

I walked off into the gloom. All alone. Under a bridge I came upon a swampy puddle. Water! It tasted brackish, of algae, oil, and withered leaves. I drank it in thirsty gulps, filled the containers, and waited for my comrades.

The roads got worse. In front of us the forest rose like a black wall. Deep mud slowed us down. The exhausted, unwatered, and unfed horses reeled in the traces. We groped our way forward through the night. A late, pale moon rose over the treetops. Corduroy roads alternated with sand and boggy track. First-growth trees, birches, alders, and firs adjoined small clearings, patches of heather and moorland. We lost our way.

We parked our guns and vehicles at the edge of a clearing, spread tarpaulins and blankets on the wet grass, and slept. The next morning we went on, and the march got a little easier in the blowing light. Then once again the sun burned over the leaves and twigs, dried the sweat on our brows, evaporated the dew, and turned the air to steam. We picked cranberries and cooled our hands in moss, moistened our wrists with swamp water, watered the horses, and finally went off the road altogether. We rested in the swampy forest at Bryansk and slept away the day.

Evening. The rain drummed on the leaves, and impenetrable darkness spread everywhere. We traveled to our new position along narrow forest paths, past collapsed barns, until finally the tangle of trees lightened. In front of us was a plain with tall steppe grass, weeds, and bushes. The shallow trenches ran along the edge of the forest opposite. We couldn't see them. With damp hands we put up a tent in the rain and warmed up a few cans of food on the open fire. No sentries were posted; no one knew from where the Russians might be coming, whether there was danger, or whether we were camped in the middle of no-man's-land.

The next noon we returned to the resting place from the day before. We were not yet on call, but slowly the extent of the calamity at Orel began to dawn on us. We cursed that we were to be sacrificed for a bit of swampy woodland.

We moved into a blockhouse. Unfinished timber walls supported a roof of fir branches, rushes, and grass. We stuffed moss into the chinks, brought in grass and ferns to bed down on, lit a candle, and were finally able to write.

State of alarm. We heard shots and their multiple echoes among the trees. A machine gun clattered into the branches over our heads. We dropped to the floor and listened. Eerie quiet.

We undertook a scouting trip into the strange, perilous wood. Moonlight shone on the paths; slimy, rotting wood glowed spectrally; shadows danced menacingly in the wind. Drowsy birdcalls rang out; a screech owl screamed into space; bats flickered through the foliage. Twigs cracked. Fleeing deer crashed through the undergrowth. The night was full of noises and dangers.

We stopped in a clearing, rifles at the ready, listened for a long time, and stared at the dimly illumined grass. Nothing but the night wind singing its monotonous song. The leaves rustled. Then we jumped; shudders chased through us: fleeing footfall, the cracking of branches, whispered conversation. We picked up a Russian word. We dived into the underbrush, stood back to back, and watched. Our eyes hurt with tense looking, but nothing moved anymore. The enemy was everywhere and nowhere. We went back. My palpitations eased, and before long I was asleep in the blockhouse, trusting to my good angel and my fate. The adventurer was well looked after.

We made ourselves a little more comfortable. From our shelter we listened to the wind sing and the rain bash on the roof, collected berries by day, and stood at night leaning against tree trunks, shielded by bushes, and, as if one with them, watched perfectly still, staring into the dark or the moony depths of the forest, and slept uneasily, pursued by dreams. I read Rilke and Claudius, and at last I felt something like a yearning for my own life: books, music, and peace.

I collected mosses and lichens, swamp flowers, and fallen leaves. Wasps and flies swarmed; piratical hornets zoomed across the paths. In the evenings the mosquitoes danced their complicated rounds, in accordance with some obscure law. Under tall pines and beeches, firs and birches, rare oaks spread their crowns and established their lebensraum. Alders, rowans, and sycamores struggled for light; hazel thickets, willows, buckthorns lined clearings and paths. Under them grew ferns, raspberries, and reeds. Moss, heather, and lichen covered the ground. Small otters whisked through the grass; ants traveled on invisible highways through rotten pine needles, last year's foliage, and humus. A smell of decomposition, rot, resin, and warm earth, of leaves, berries, and moldering wood was carried on the soft breeze. Morels lurked in the gloom, puffballs scattered their black dust, and fungi sat in the crooks of dead trees. Sometimes I would find a cadaver in the bushes, thick with flies, while burying beetles did their work on the underside. I was overcome with nausea.

Sometimes I would lie there for hours on end, dreaming, watching a solitary moth, studying the sun flashing in the leaves, listening to the voices of the wood, thinking of summers of childhood and the magical woods of Darss. Here there was no pure joie de vivre, no unmixed beauty, no ravishing promenade. Everything was hostile and unfamiliar: the flowers and trees, earth and water, just like the whole immense country. It was oppressive, sad, silent, conducive to melancholy and gloom. It drained your soul and gave it back empty. I had no home here; I was just a guest, uninvited and tired; the spirits avoided me; nothing spoke to me. And for all that, I thought I belonged here more than I did at home. It was a strange life I was living.

Our position near Batogovo was given up in turn. An unfinished bunker was left behind. We moved out one moonless night. Darkness waved in the wood; only above the broad road was there a slightly paler strip of sky, where stars sometimes appeared. Thick mud covered the tarmac road, interspersed with stretches of corduroy road, which made the horses' loads feel a little lighter. Hour upon hour we dragged ourselves through the morass, plunging into potholes, bashing into trees and branches that smacked across our sightless eyes. In the end we let ourselves be dragged along by the vehicles. We were all done up.

Morning broke with flying lights. A large clearing opened up: plain, expanse of hills, endless forest on the horizon. Silvery light lay over the quiet landscape. The lingering coolness of the air was a memory of the night. In the fine haze, birches and firs rose by the roadside, magically beautiful, filigree work of great spirituality and distinction.

My tiredness disappeared. I saw the muted play of colors before daybreak, the mild beauty of the shapes, and suddenly I was once more in love with life and drank in the splendor and beauty of the earth with grateful eyes. Wheresover fate might move me, however difficult the time might be, however miserable existence might appear to be, as long as I could sate my gaze on the plenitude of wonders and listen to the thousand voices of Mother Earth, no single day was wasted. Every hour had its own secret meaning and value. Unforgettable images came to me and stilled the hunger of my spirit. Dreams filled in what duress had kept from being realized. Unconsidered things germinated, and great events awoke the slumbering spirit. I needed only to walk, and life was mine: great, impalpable life that, like a beautiful and terrible adventure, grew and, in the hazardousness of war, came to its full charm and loveliness, and filled me to bursting, but didn't surfeit, enclosing me in the great circle of being and transformation, along with the grasses and the wild beasts.

This hour before daybreak returned me to my affirmation and my amen, to my fate and to the whole world. I prayed that I might never lose it. The whole landscape filled with light; every little leaf was gilded; every blade of grass radiated warmth. I was proud of my perilous life, of everything I had survived and endured, collected and thought. To live life in its entirety, with all my senses and all my intellectual energy: Nothing else mattered. And for a long time my pride carried me through the arduous days.

We rested. Then we marched through an idyllic landscape of villages and fields, into the evening. I still dream of the pale green foliage of morning and the silvery gray birches in twilight. We passed Verkhi and put up our tents by the millpond. We homeless men soon felt at home anywhere. Rain showers blew over us. The candle flickered in the draft. We read our letters, wrapped them in our wet blankets, and stood sentry in cloudburst and night.

The next day the forest took us in again, lighter now in the mild September sun. On mud roads we marched through a glade at eventide. Two hanged men swayed on a protruding branch. A musty smell of decomposition hung around their stiff forms. Their faces were swollen and bluish, contorted to grimaces. The flesh was coming away from the nails of their tied hands; yellow-brown ichor dribbled out of their eyes and crusted on their cheeks, on which the stubble had continued to grow. One soldier took their picture; another gave them a swing with his stick. Partisans. We laughed and moved off, along corduroy roads in the broad-leaved wood. Nightfall found us by the edge of the wood; we didn't know the positions and sent a couple of men out ahead as scouts. They were gone for many hours. Missing. They never came back, and we found no trace of them.

Stars shimmered through the birch tops. Night coolness drizzled down on us. We shivered with cold, hunger, and fatigue, but no one dared sleep.

I sat propped against a tree trunk and listened to the idle conversations. The voices softened; the words blurred to strange sounds. Fantasy wove her will-o'-the-wisp textures around things half understood. Snatches of dream melodies went by me, and then all was quiet.

I awoke. Alone, insouciantly fallen asleep in partisan country. I got a shock. With hurried strides, I followed the path, looking for tracks of our vehicles, but without my rifle, which I'd left behind. It had barely grown lighter. An order had come through, and the others had forgotten about me. I caught up with them at the edge of the forest.

The light vacillated in the east. Ahead of us the landscape climbed slowly, pastureland between dunes with exiled Mediterranean pines, sank into a valley, and rose on the opposite side with brown-singed heathland, steeply up to small conifer woods. That was where the Russians were.

As it darkened, and in the cover afforded by some evening mist, we found some protective bushes and a half-made bunker. We concealed the gun and our wagon in the brush, spread out our blankets, and slept, indifferent with tiredness, with no sentries, just behind the trench, on the road, like Gypsies.

Only the next morning did we find our designated position. It was among sand dunes near the front line. A young pinewood kept us out of sight, and there was a bunker there as well. We always had an undemanding home waiting for us, to live in and sleep in and one day to die in. We shared out the last of our tobacco and smoked cheerily. We had shelter against the weather, had pallets, a desk to write on, could set up our stove and no longer needed to freeze. And when wine and champagne were brought out in the evening, why, then our cups were running over.

The Russians attacked in the morning mist and soon sobered us up. A brief drumfire wrecked the trenches in the sand, and the attackers entered Pavlovka, a deserted village on the height next to us. Our infantry beat them back, and by midday all was quiet again.

Quiet days passed. I wrote letters and sat reading in the sun, performed my tasks, gathering firewood and fetching water in no-man's-land, because the well there was nearer than the one behind our lines. Often we encountered Russian soldiers with buckets. Then we fired at them, a few bullets whistled past us, and we went back. After an hour we undertook the unnecessary risk again and took hand grenades with us, but we didn't use them. It would be all too easy for the Russians to surround us and take us prisoner; a chance bullet could hit us. We didn't care.

We challenged destiny, as if to force a decision for or against us and our lives, return or death. But all we did was cause unnecessary excitement, and we didn't take our secret hopes very seriously anymore. We weren't sure if we could live without the war and without Russia. Even when a windy Sunday awoke my yearning for Darss, putting me in mind of love affairs and games on the beach, I still felt like an actor playing impossible parts.

We were in a sort of berserk humor then. We mocked death and danger, distorted things, and drove all thoughts into the grotesque. Our scouting trips to the well became like boyish pranks, and we liked to annoy the Russians by parading our steel helmets over the rim of the trench. We dressed ourselves in comedy and irony, toyed with ridiculous turns of phrase, and came to depend on our silly hysterics.

Under this mask, though, a tragedy went over; an inner calamity took its implacable course. I drifted into a spiritual vacuum. The last of my values collapsed; goodness, nobility, beauty perished; my high spirits left me. The armor of apathy with which I had covered myself against terror, horror, fear, and madness, which had saved me from suffering and screaming, crushed any tender stirrings within me, snapped off the green shoots of hope, faith, and love of my fellow men, and turned my heart to stone. I was in decline, and I mocked myself for it.

Often I was taken by a limitless sadness. I scrabbled through the debris of my youth and felt desperate that I couldn't get the ashes of my existence to burst into new flame. I strayed along the frontier, wiped out my memories of sea, music, and poetry, almost forgot my own name, and gave myself over to the shadows, the spectral existence of my mask, the mask of the laughing soldier. The wells were dry for a long time, it was a time of drought, apostasy swallowed up my stars, and I rejected my God. I was shipwrecked by my fate, tossed onto a deserted shore, with infinities ahead of me, the broken bridges of the past behind me, and, among a thousand roads, not one to lead me home.

Frost-candied meadows, woods, and hills didn't speak to me. I no longer understood their language. Only occasionally a wild yearning blazed up in me, and I was afraid that these wounds would never be healed. Not only paradise but also hell was lost to us. Never had I felt myself so much of an adventurer in no-man's-land.

Nothing new occurred. Everything was repetition: danger and death, flight and wandering, fear, suffering, hope, and loneliness, and plains, forests, fogs, and the heat of the sun. I had experienced them all so many, many times before. My life kept spiraling back to the same point. Emptiness and fullness alternated as formerly flood and ebb tide by the sea. At the beginning and ending of everything was the void.

Nothing meant anything: not the war and not peace either. Freedom would never come, and a return home was just a dream. Mankind would continue to dance around work and bread, and even the ghostly dance of the fallen seemed to revolve around the golden calf. We, though, despised the men who stayed at home and hadn't experienced death, battle, and danger as we had, who hadn't put themselves through the worst—which was what made life so precious to us and often so shocking. There was a desperate pride in our position.

At the same time, I bore in mind that I was fighting men I didn't hate, who were never enemies to me, who in their destiny were more like my brothers; and that I was only trying to perform an imposed duty, not unlike a monk serving strange idols yet putting all his devotion and passion into his service and this order. What made us great wasn't what we did but what we suffered. It was God's great game, and we had to be content to be figures in it.

The world was wide. None of it went to waste. But the great

life that was bred in war remained an illusion, a projection of death.

In this way, I wobbled between interpretations, seeing significance and contradiction, always in uncertainty and always in night.

The forest position was vacated without a fight. We moved out in early moonlight and marched into hopelessness. It got cold. Fogs ghosted over the meadows, blew out of the trees with a dark cavernous smell. In the distance the flares of the rear guard went dazzling up. We lost our way in the foggy land. We struggled through streams, fields, and dense undergrowth, toward higher ground, and, after looking a long time, found a forest track that led us back to the tarmac road.

Russian planes dropped phosphorus around us. The landscape was lit up bright as day, and we saw marching troops, as far as anyone could see. Our horses got tired. We lagged behind. There was only darkness between us and the enemy. Silence surrounded us. We stopped and listened. I had an auditory hallucination of bells and ethereal music and listened deeply. Like a bowl, I opened myself to the night, and the mysterious chiming filled me to the brim and flowed on out into the silent world. I suddenly gave a jump. The others weren't hearing anything. It was all going on inside me.

We got to a bridge. Ready to blow. With savage shouts, we succeeded in driving the horses across the river, dragged the guns ourselves, and pushed the wagons. A mine, laid by our sappers, blew up drovers, horses, and the first of the guns. We didn't care. We understood that no one was expecting us to get through. Given up, left to our own devices, we hastened through no-man's-land. Repeatedly we stepped up the pace, even as our legs were quitting on us.

Mortar fire blocked our way. We waited, but the Russians didn't charge. Then we bundled together the last of our strength and charged behind the bolting horses into a hail of iron, earth, and tree boughs. We reached the last bridge.

Alarmed soldiers motioned to us to go back. The fuse was already lit; no one on the other side dared go up and put it out. We stampeded across, standing on limbers and carts, shouting and whipping the horses, and on the other side hurled ourselves to the ground. The explosion covered us with splinters and lumps of clay, tore the air from our lungs, and scattered the horses. No one was hurt.

We soon managed to round up the exhausted animals, and in the first light we reached the outer line of defense, set up the guns in the frosty pastureland, found straw, and slept.

We set off before it was evening. Tracks, roads, always straight ahead. As a rear guard, we paused in an incinerated village. Somewhere ahead of us was a base; that was all we knew.

We carted planks and beams to the glowing embers of a house, stoked up a mighty fire, lay down in the hot ashes, and slept. No sentries watched over us. From time to time the cold awakened us, and we chucked fresh wood into the fire, stared into the flickering flames, wiped the dust and ashes off our haggard faces, and went to sleep again.

Roused by the whinnying of the horses, we saw the last members of the rear guard creeping past and joined them. I felt unwell and lay down on the transom, fell asleep on the gun, and woke only as we were bouncing over fields and stopping in a clump of alders. We found a spring, drank the ice-cold water, and rested.

In the evening, on the Bolva, we found only trenches and a fire site, no bunker. In a wood adjacent to a defile, we dug out a hole in the earth, laid tarpaulins over the entrance, and waited for vehicles to bring timber and brackets.

Through a gap in the bushes we saw the trench and a wide expanse of brown swampland in the fog, with the forest of Bryansk in the distance. That night the flares went both ways; we listened to the rumbling of tanks already having crossed the Bolva and unquietly waited for the day.

At around noon a sudden drumfire from tanks, mortars, and artillery pieces began. It seemed to concentrate on the trenches and then brushed us in the hinterland. We huddled in our hole in the ground, barely protected. Splinters trickled down; clouds and smoke and dust obscured our vision. A splinter struck me high on the temple. I saw the blood dripping into the sand but was too excited to feel any pain. I got myself bandaged up and stayed with my taciturn comrades.

No one dared look out. The Russians charged; we were in the focus of their mortar fire, listening to their "URRAH," unable to get to our gun, the path to which was open, and a chaotic scene of smoke and dust.

A tank drove past us, and we retired to the end of the defile. The heavy weapons fire continued, machine guns hammered into it, and very nearby already, the short bursts of submachine guns.

The scene resembled a boiling cauldron of sunshine, whirling clods of earth, and gunpowder smoke. A couple of rifle shots next to me made me jump. A few paces behind me, a Russian collapsed; others were creeping through the undergrowth.

We leaped up and ran up the hill, through their wild firing and the occasional shellburst, one man with no boots, I with my gleaming white bandage. We caught our breath in a hollow for a few seconds. I was panting, my head seemed about to burst, my heart was banging away, but the Russians were still coming.

We crossed a ridge, slowly, too exhausted to mind the danger. A few hundred yards to the side of us, we could see long lines of Russians attacking a little village, and in the distance we saw our infantry in full flight. We discussed what to do and decided to run the gauntlet of Russian fire; there was no other choice. Calmly we went on and climbed down into a narrow gorge, listened, pricked up our ears for the enemy, and lay on our bellies on the wet ground, cooled our faces and hands, and drank greedily.

We pulled ourselves back up on bushes and thorns and saw the Russians leaving the village they had only just taken. Withdrawing. The line ahead of us was occupied again, only where we had left the gun there was a wide gap. It stood there untouched in the evening light.

It was getting dark, and the five of us went over onto a counteroffensive. Once again we crossed the gorge and charged across the ridge. Machine guns forced us to the ground. One by one, we leaped up, dropped to the ground again, and next to us the bullets smacked into the grass. We could feel the air pressure. We were waiting for darkness.

With bloodcurdling cries, we threw ourselves upon our gun. A little later, reservists rolled up the trench and cleaned the area. I rode to the doctor, had my wound cleaned and dabbed with iodine, and returned to my comrades. The night was deathly still.

In the morning we buried the dead man, a young Tatar, who was still clutching his submachine gun in his stiff hands. We made a hole next to the corpse, dragged him into it, and bent his stiff limbs till all of him went in. On his throat and chest we saw the dried blood of his wounds. When we moved him, his neck swung back. With a gurgle, a slime of blood and drool spilled out of his mouth. A stench rose, flies swerved around the body, and shuddering with nausea, we quickly closed up the hole.

There wasn't time to give him a cross, just the tump of earth to indicate that a dead soldier lay there, fallen, so that we might live. But he haunted me for a long time to come.

Marching orders. In frantic haste, we loaded the cart with ammunition and baggage, put the horses to, and marched, marched.

This was the way defeated troops marched, to avoid encirclement. We didn't know where we were going.

We marched, marched.

Uncertain Wanderings

FLIGHT

We marched through moonlit forests, over endless roads, plains, and hills, till the day dawned. Then we stopped to rest, slept among thistles and corn stooks, and in the dusk shot off the rest of our ammunition at a deserted village, just to lighten the carts a little.

Ruined villages, debris, and char marked our way. Behind us the last houses went up in flames, woods burned on the horizon, munitions dumps were blown up, and flares, shells, and bombs went up like fireworks into the night sky. By our side were other columns, occasionally the populations of evacuated villages with their carts and animals or else dragging their households on their backs. Old and young women, children, pregnant women, single men, barefoot, in ripped shoes, with sacking wrapped around their feet. We overtook herds of cattle and sheep. An endless column stretched backward and forward, making all the time for the west. In some places the forest was already burning, a last barrier against the advancing Russians.

The dawn burned like a planetary fire, with the terrible force of beauty. We got across the Desna. Our little band found itself in a great mass of fugitives. Women, prisoners, and soldiers were working on positions that would surely fall into Russian hands the very next day. It started to rain and didn't stop. We marched and marched. The day passed. Night fell on muddy, churned-up roads. Still, we marched on.

We found three hours of sleep in a ravaged village. Onward. We set off again at midnight. Day brightened. Low hill country, expanse of swamps, meadows, fields, and pastures. Very slowly the landscape altered its aspect. We barely took in the rich villages and their beauty in the last light of September. Our progress became a reeling, almost a crawling. We clung on to the cart, deposited rifles and bread sacks in it, let the trembling horses drag us forward, while our legs mechanically moved on.

No more sleep the next night. One man shot himself out of despair and exhaustion. Others remained behind, disappeared; some went on ahead on vehicles and were lost that way. Panic drove us on; uncertainty choked us. Marching and marching.

Late the next morning, we got to Pochep, to be put on trains. The Russians were still pressing; Pochep was due to be abandoned the very next day. We waited timorously, at the end of our strength. We had covered more than ninety miles in two days and three nights.

That was our flight.

We waited to be entrained. Armored cars, assault guns drove up the ramps. Trucks without engines, shot-up artillery pieces, useless tractors were loaded up, wedged tight, and made fast, as train after train rolled westward. There was no room for us. The railwaymen were drunk. Train drivers and firemen slept on the tenders. We plundered the stores and canteens, loaded our cart with boxes of wine and spirits, looted tobacco and cigarettes, put on new uniforms, brought sweets, writing things, and soap out of the basements, where the charges of dynamite had already been put down, and we started to drink. Most of it went bad, was destroyed, or fell into the hands of the victorious Russians. Carts full of planks, beams, coal, and scrap iron were saved. We had to march. Our new destination was Unecha.

We were in despair. Marching and marching. Noonday sun burned down on dusty roads. We followed the tarmac. Then we mutinied.

With not many comrades, I climbed onto a slowly moving truck. Other units melted away; only the drivers remained with their horses. The rest of us got away. No orders were capable of keeping us exhausted men back, and the desire to live broke out in us once more. We rode, and we asked no questions.

The wind cooled our brows, and not until evening did we jump off. Endless columns of motor vehicles were dragging west on the tarmac road; heavily laden troops marched more slowly on the side roads. We rested by the roadside and looked on the map for the village of Staroselye, where we were supposed to overnight.

Slowly, five exhausted soldiers with bleeding and inflamed feet, we followed a track through grassy hills and peaceful fields into the evening. The cool and silent country was already asleep. Lights blinked in a village on a hill. A girl pointed us the way.

It was getting dark by the time we saw the first houses of Staroselye. We ransacked them for eggs, butter, and lard, oblivious to the amazement of the women and the men's mothers. We settled in one brightly lit room, drew the curtains, got the women to light a fire for us on the stove, to fix us supper. Reluctantly and slowly they obeyed, muttering to themselves. It was an odd feeling. We had no weapons. There were voices outside, whispering but excited.

I drew my knife and went out. A group of young men were standing by the window, listening. They looked at me and asked in broken German if we meant to torch the village. No. But they didn't believe me.

With heart pounding, I went out onto the street. It was night, dimly lit by a few stars and a pale crescent moon. Whistles sounded in the dark; shouts rang out from the bushes. I went back inside and reported.

Three of my comrades crept through the garden, listened out, and caught the sounds of an excited meeting. All of them were young men with sticks and scythes, now setting off in the direction of our house.

The three men hurried back and told us. We had already broken up the chairs and other furniture, and armed ourselves with clubs and metal bars, and taken our bayonets in our hands.

Now we came charging out and hurled ourselves against the garden fence, crashed through it onto the grass, and raced down the hill. Shots rang out after us. We ran down the track and stopped only when we reached the bottom of the hill from which we had first seen the lights. In that village we found lodging, soldiers, and something to eat. Our sleep was uneasy, but the partisans didn't bother us.

I was troubled by dreams, dreams of flight, imprisonment, and death. Earlier I would sometimes see only myself wandering in the foggy land, and the spice of adventure affected these fights and travels too. But now the demons chased me through torture and flight, and these dreams seemed not to end.

Early in the morning we returned to the tarmac road. A truck took us along as far as Unecha. I sat on the fender in the wind, saw meadows and stubble fields slip by, woods, shrubs, and villages, and I felt a blissful intoxication. The adventure of being on the road, relying on myself, and free, the ride west, and my near escapes of the past night transported me into a mood of exuberant joie de vivre.

A feeble sun lit the plain; the wind tugged at my hair; my cheeks and brows were seared by the air and dust. The experience of velocity was translated into an inner surge. For a few hours I was free, a drunken traveler in the unknown, a little closer to home, and I enjoyed my liberty like an opiate. I didn't feel like a soldier, but like a human being, a vagrant abroad in a wonderful world.

The factories and storehouses of Unecha appeared behind thin trees. Railway tracks. Freight trains going by. In the evening, we arrived, collected ourselves, and hooked up with other members of our platoon. More turned up all the time. We learned that some had already been put on trains in Klinzy and that onward transport was expected tomorrow.

That evening we entrained. We weren't punished and barely scolded. Our comrades treated us to vodka and red wine. I have to say, I missed my freedom and the adventurousness of being on the road.

Slowly we headed toward Gomel, seeing always the same thing: harvested fields in a storm, smoke clouds on the horizon. Russia was turning into a depopulated, smoking, burning, wreckage-strewn desert, and the war behind the front bothered me still more, because those it affected were noncombatants. I was partly responsible for this devastation and the grief it brought the people, responsible like all the nameless victims, like all the soldiers. I had almost forgotten that there was anything besides war and flight. I no longer dreamed of going home.

Ahead of us a bridge had been blown up. The train stopped on the middle of the line, in an endless chain of transports. Squads of sappers worked feverishly to rebuild the bridge. It wasn't quickly enough. Partisans took the villages around, the Red Army was approaching, and the last trains were already on the front line. Mortars shelled us, and we made ready to defend ourselves.

Meanwhile the traveling life continued. We ate up our booty from Pochep, broke into provision wagons and looted them, carried out boxes of sugar, wine, preserves, and meat, spent the day roasting and boiling, and the different kitchens vied with one another as to who could make the best dishes. We wrote letters we weren't able to send and drank far into the night.

We sang over claret and liqueurs, vodka and rum, plunged into intoxication like doomed men, talked drunkenly about sex and science, reeled by the railroad cars, sat outside over campfires, were made ill by the cheap spirits and the sudden rich diet, and carried on anyway, made grotesque speeches about war and peace, grew melancholy, talked about our lovelornness and homesickness, started laughing again, and went on drinking, whooped and skipped over the rails, danced in the cars, and fired into the air, made a Russian woman prisoner dance naked for us, greased her tits with boot polish, got her as drunk as we were, and sobered up only when we reached Gomel after five days. By order, the rest of the alcohol was destroyed. We rode, via Zhlobin, Mogilev, and Orsha, to Gorki. There we detrained.

The flight was over; now began the trench war to hold the line of the Dnieper.

THE BATTLE

October sun decked the country in pallid gold. A cool wind blew over hills and fields, the grass yellowed, the blue air was redolent of damp earth, and a clear day passed. We were marching to the front. In the evening we rested in Andrychów. We lay around a fire of turf, wood, and straw. Ominous-looking clouds gathered at nightfall, and the sun sank behind the gardens in an orgy of purple, cinnabar, crimson, violet, and gold.

The fire burned lower. We wrapped ourselves more tightly in our coats and put up our collars. Russian planes were bombing the village in phosphorescent light. We had many dead and wounded, and most of the horses were lost. But at midnight we set out.

The darkness made it harder to find a way through the swampy hollows and over hills where the winter crop had begun to sprout. It was some time before the fires of Luki gave us a misty light to walk by.

Hard behind the trench, after we had lost our way and in our exhaustion fallen asleep on the gun, we found a fire site and a hole in the ground to sleep in. We walked down the trench. Tarpaulins had been made fast to the walls, masking holes where a soldier might be asleep on thin straw. The night frost glittered on the ground. The sunny days brought with them a fresh wind, and the evenings damp fog. The defenders often watched through the night here. Their guns rested in narrow rills; a small depression in the clay contained food, ammunition, and smokes.

There was one more base ahead of us. Calmly we carted up beams and boards, built us a bunker, and slept, barely watched, while north of Lenino a battle was already raging, and Russian storm troops appeared at night in front of our barbed wire. The front was quiet. We felt quiet as well. Time dribbled through our exhausted hands like sand; we could see no specks of gold in it.

We were tormented by lice and scabies. We went off to be deloused and slathered ourselves with sulfur ointment. Not before time, we were given clean shirts. The ones we were wearing had gone black. And so we moved into our winter quarters.

Drumfire ravaged the trenches and woke us from our tangled dreams. Shells from all sorts of weapons were going up, and their detonation, impact, and whining approach made a single monotonous hurricane of noise. We threw ourselves into the deepest trenches. Earth and shrapnel struck our steel helmets. Even I replaced my forage cap. Only for seconds at a time did we dare look out into the fog-hung no-man's-land. Nothing there stirred. Hours passed. The bombardment was unabating. We noticed we were at its focus. The Russians were already charging. Wave after wave of them flowed out into the valley and soon dipped out of our sight. We launched a few shells into the places where they were massed, plunged away from the gun, lay in wait, hazarded another race against death, all until night instituted a pause in hostilities. The Russians had broken through half a mile to the side of us.

It froze. The full moon rose bloodred and didn't go down till day began to break. A veiled yellow sun rose over the Russian positions. The strongpoint in front of us was vacated. A little heap of ragged, miserable, and sleepless soldiers fled to us and hid behind the trenches, sitting exhausted and crushed in a gully, and seemed still to be staring at what they'd been through.

The shelling recommenced. The battle resumed. An inferno of fire, steel, and blood. At about noon the drumfire intensified further. The Russians were building on their success of the previous day. Tanks and artillery pieces arrived too late and were shot down; vainly our dive-bombers attacked the enemy's lines. Flamethrowers failed. Nothing could save us from the enemy numbers. One company withdrew from the trench, and two of our guns were lost.

The Russians drove their wedge farther into our hinterland. Our reserves were being bled dry, even before any counterattack could be mounted. There was no help to come. We wrote farewell letters and waited to die.

The line was given up section by section. Corpses piled up. Behind the mounds of dead, the desperate living fought on.

Smashed by direct hits, wounded, suffering nervous collapse, my comrades quit. As if by a miracle, I escaped the shells time and again and became light-headed. Nothing seemed to matter. No one was in communication with us anymore. We didn't try anything, didn't fret, just waited for the end. We kept up a strange veneer of order and calm, smoked, ate. Then we fled in panic through the choked trenches, taking nothing with us. The Russians were still a ways off, but no one thought of resisting. No one had any strength or willpower left. It wasn't death or danger or the enemy that scared us. But as no help came and neither smoke projectors nor artillery supervened, we felt we couldn't do anything on our own behalf either. Shells smashed down on the overcrowded trenches. We jumped out and slowly ambled up the slope through machine-gun fire. Everything was a matter of indifference, and today was as good a day to die on—or, if we were spared, to be wounded—as the next.

I helped a comrade get to a doctor. He made it home.

We were put to the sword like sacrificial victims. This wasn't fighting anymore; it was butchery. In the course of brief counterthrusts, we found our missing in little pieces, and we didn't take any prisoners either. We defended ourselves only until an opportunity arose for flight. We weren't fighting.

But that night we went on a scouting mission into no-man's-land. We came down from our defensive line on the crest of the hill, climbed down into the gully, and crawled up the facing slope toward our gun. Trenches and positions lay abandoned in the darkness. We listened. Nothing but the blood pounding at our temples. We pulled the gun into the gully, got help, and lugged it up the hill. A group of stragglers passed us, going back. The last. None spoke. The wheels dragged on the grass. A few shells whirred over our heads. We took a breather.

A pair of us went back again. Slowly the Russian flares got

closer. They were moving forward along a broad front, into untenanted space. We stopped at our bunker. Muffled voices sounded somewhere, not near. It was a suicidal adventure. I lay down with my rifle, safety catch off, and my pistol in hand. My comrade fetched our bread sacks and packs, brought the blankets out. We made up our packs. The voices grew louder. They were very near now, and we could make out Russian words. We picked up our things and ran into the gully. Shouts and rapid fire from submachine guns followed us. Shadows, outlines loomed over the heights; a fireworks display of flares lit the scene as bright as day. We ran on, tumbled into craters and ditches, stumbled over dead, and finally got back to our new position.

With a few more shells, the battle ended the next day. We were saved, or rather, we had been conditionally reprieved for an unknown period.

Quiet days passed. There were the aftereffects of terror. I kept seeing in front of me the wall of fire, smoke, earth, and dust that we had lived and fought through. There was no escaping these visions, and whoever got away with his life would wear the burn scars of those hours as long as he lived. I had once again experienced the war in its full horror, as an apotheosis of devastation and death.

The blood dried in the clay and disappeared underfoot. The dead were buried. But after this experience it wasn't possible for life to go on; no one who had been through this could ever be a human and a son of God anymore. Yet things went on; they had to be borne and gotten over.

My will to live reawakened. My resources of mind and spirit stirred once more, as though replenished from some mysterious source. I wiped those days and nights from my life. Buried them deep, as though they had never been. I built a bridge across the chasm of that time and started a new life on the other side.

We were found a calmer position. For a few days we had quiet behind the front.

Once more we walked in fog and through the night. We hardly noticed one another. We were shadows, conducting spectral conversations and heading into the light. The air was heavy with moisture and cool, and the brassy music of the front rolled back to us. The night was without danger, and our position was good, a long way behind the firing trenches, a warm and fully built bunker. And there we moved in.

A few rainy days went by. At the beginning of November it snowed for the first time. The howling gale drove the wet snow over the grass. Our stove was burning. We listened to the crackling of the wood as it crumbled, and the humming of the wind. The snow on the hill melted before it got light. We grew quiet.

A fire, a hut in the rainy country, were always there for the wanderer. God saw to the beasts of the field, and he gave us his tender blessings at the right time. Battles and death recurred, but there were pauses periodically as well. Out of danger and pain, new ore came to the soul, and it was up to us to smelt it first into steel and then into gold. Even if we buried the faithless stars in iron coffins, still we carried light within us.

A village was on fire in the night, but the stars were quiet above the dancing flames. I was out and lost my way among the trenches. Without realizing it, I was wandering through no-man's-land, and I was close to the Russian trenches before the red tracer from enemy machine guns showed me the way back. But everything slipped by me with that dreamy mixture of objectivity and confusion that registers things like a mirror but doesn't grasp them.

Quiet. The quiet did us no good. We were still wired after the battle and needed activity, finding it only in brandy and card games. We listened to the primal song of the gale and pondered.

In this damned time, it was the best thing to be a soldier and at least stand squarely in the midst of this life. I felt in tune with my fate in a way I couldn't justify. I no longer sought to fend off the inevitable, did my duty with a certain pleasure, and was surprised at myself. The memory of music and poems made me aware of the grotesqueness of my soldier's life in Russia, like some inner laughter, and I guessed that with the next drumfire, all this would burst like a soap bubble.

But then the comedy acquired a deeper level. The war had become such an elemental planetary occurrence that everything else seemed fugitive, like froth and smoke, hoarfrost in the sunlight. Freedom, poesy, and song took up merely symbolic space, beyond reality. I had to be a soldier, inside as out, in order to exist in this reality of killing and dying; to keep a purchase on this ravaged earth, I had to die forlornly.

That was what I thought when it was quiet and I couldn't fathom myself. Suddenly I yearned once more for mobility and travels into the unknown. It was like the return of hope and desire. I regained belief in my destiny. I found trust in life and youthful confidence and awaited whatever might come to pass with equanimity. I waited for adventure.

And my secret desire was fulfilled.

GYPSIES ON THE ROAD

One dark, rainy night we moved out. We headed toward fresh calamities, privations, pains, and adventures. In Koyuchow and Sukino, we had lived almost as in peacetime. The turn of events could bring only bitter news. But I was pleased. I kept faith with my strange soldierliness. I might be an adventurer in no-man's-land, a shuttlecock of fate, but my inner self was in balance. The hopelessness of the war, the futility of my wanderings, the despair at any change, fear of the blessings of a return to home and peace, disgust at the insane crimes of humanity, all combined to make me see the last possibility of a completed life in death in Russia. So I moved out with confused spirits.

We marched in a northwesterly direction. I gave myself to the melancholy beauty of autumnal landscapes. Rain fell; the tarmac turned to mud, freezing over at night and thawing out again by day. We crossed the Dnieper and found ourselves on the western bank of the river. Ahead of us was the roaring of the battle along the road from Smolensk to Minsk. No one knew where the road was taking us. It disappeared into infinity.

At Budy we spent the night in a barn. A gigantic stove was lit, but the wind came sweeping in. Stars flashed through the thatched roof, and snow trickled in. We pulled on our winter gear, which was an improvement on the previous year's, drank rum and champagne, slept a few hours, and set off to look for our postings in the gloaming. We got there in the dark, moved into a bunker, and slept in scraps, continually awoken by the fiendish concert of smoke projectors, surprise fire, and sentry duty.

But the great battle was almost over. We captured a village and freed a platoon that had dug in there, waiting to be rescued or starved. There was no Russian counterthrust. It was only a few late skirmishes that we caught. The weather grew milder. We lay on pallets, sang songs in all kinds of languages, and got drunk every night. We forgot our worries and our lives. They were worth only a tired tossing away.

New position. We marched back along the road. Rain showers brushed the land. We sang and walked, buzzy and optimistic on rum and champagne, and accepted the adventures ahead with an alcoholic equanimity. We were put on trains at Olyustino, spent the night in a freight car over cards and wine, and got out at Staraye Bykhov. We followed the road through mud, rain, and snow and recrossed the Dnieper.

Like men condemned to drown, we stared at the water, measured its depth with apprehensive eyes, shivered, and marched on, dully submissive to our fate, tired of war and the lot of being forever at the easternmost point on the front.

We reached Selez, a village that had been recaptured only that morning. Russian bazookas and machine guns still lined the street, and the dead lay beside their weapons. We waited for night, huddled shivering around a fire, but it wasn't till morning that we moved off to our posts.

We marched through a snowy wood, and stopping to rest once, I fell asleep under a bush. When I awoke, the others had moved off, having taken prisoner a few Russian stragglers who had surrendered after a few shots.

We were approaching the main fighting line. Shells came out to greet us on the road. We found a wounded man, abandoned by his comrades. By twos we carried him into cover and bandaged him up while the tank shells crashed, and earth and shrapnel fell on top of us. His face was yellow, screaming, contorted by pain. The veins and sinews in his thigh were exposed, and his blood froze on our hands. He died. We chased after the others.

In a blizzard-black night, we put the gun into position. We found several earth holes in the vicinity, just wide and deep enough to take a pair of men lying on their sides. We put up tarpaulins over them, rolled ourselves into our blankets, and slept. No one on watch. The rain pattered down. It dripped into our holes. Thin snow covered the tarpaulins, was melted off by our breathing, and dribbled down the walls. We awoke in a puddle. Soaked and freezing, we staggered out into the fog. A mug of rum was all there was to eat or drink.

A Russian shock troop charged and remained lying in the

barrage, a long way from our guns. We built a bunker, laid a few boards over the top of it, with some straw and sand, set up a stove, and dried out our blankets, coats, and uniforms all night.

A brief drumfire from antitank guns and mortars brought us out. Dawn. Our infantry was running away; the Russians were charging down the slope ahead of us. We fired, stung by machine guns and grenades. I carried up the ammunition, saw the bullets plug into the snow in front of me. Mortar shells landed nearby. I didn't throw myself to the ground. I walked calmly and upright, as though nothing could happen to me. A counterattack repulsed the attackers, but soon they were up at us again. We shot off the last of our shells and abandoned the position. The gun was lost.

Calmly, by pairs, we walked to another gun half a mile away through machine-gun fire and isolated rifle shots. It was a matter of such indifference whether we fell here or drowned on the flight across the Dnieper. We talked about Baudelaire. Sometimes we calmly lay down, waited for the firing to abate, and went on. It was a form of madness.

The last man at the other gun was waiting for us. His face was bruised and swollen from flying clumps of earth. Cadavers lay around, and the rain poured off them. Flesh and brains were stuck to the walls of a hut. Silently we shook hands with the survivor.

We posted no sentries. Amid rain and drifting snow we fell asleep. Our own hut burned down, and we were able to rescue only our blankets and bread sacks from it. By the light of the flames, we built a bunker and tore down the beams from a barn. It was big and deep enough for us to sit and lie in.

That night I lost my way and got back very late and depressed. The following day I was transferred to a different gun and found more good comrades. We were cheek by jowl, but our worlds were compatible. I had a sense of reawakening.

Close to the trench was a little birch wood that contained our bunker. There was a glimmer of yellow from stubble fields under a blanket of white, winter wheat pushed green spikes through the snow, and on the horizon, conifer forests framed the solemn, melancholy landscape under wintry yellow light. A persistent drizzle thawed out the ground. Bit by bit, our bunker collapsed. We propped up what was left; we didn't rebuild. We were waiting for the march back; we wanted to get across the Dnieper again. That became our obsession. The river crushed us, lamed our thoughts, and became a gloomy leitmotif in all our conversations. Sometimes we paid calls on other guns, huddled close in their holes, sang, and argued the toss about war and peace, defeat and victory, and got drunk almost every night.

I felt more like a soldier than ever, but like a warrior from some future empire, a secret intellectual process that was profoundly antipathetic to war. I wore my mask, as required by the time, and dreamed of a hermit life in a vine-grown monastery cell somewhere on the edge of the world, with the din of the world only distantly audible, and standing in some intimate relation to death, but quite different. Because even the medieval dance of death seemed merciful and beautiful compared with the bare cadaver, the corpse in no-man's-land, the living dead, like myself. I was no Christian, and I had no home anywhere outside this world. I drifted through my destiny like someone deracinated, condemned to wander. On all my uncertain travels, I was never able to lean against God as against some shady tree in an oasis. My only goal remained the hope for a better life in peacetime. It would begin the moment the door of my father's house closed behind me. But in the secret chambers of my heart, I no longer believed such a moment would ever come.

This was my intellectual Advent. That was what I thought on those days of preparation, and only sometimes did I understand: I was still young, the world was open to me—at least once I was back on the western bank of the Dnieper.

It thawed, and froze again. The landscape stiffened in frost, and when I stepped out of the bunker one night, it was the first time in a long time that I saw stars overhead, stars, stars, stars. Snow sparkled, frost glittered, and profound silence lay over the earth. I was strangely happy in my Gypsy life in the forest. In December, in the open air, a good friend to trees and clouds, the wind singing in the twigs, the smell of snow, resin, and forest floor wafted up; the pine-needled earth seemed warm even in winter; I need ask for nothing, worry for nothing, could dream and hearken undisturbed. This life rejoiced the adventurer in spite of himself, and the privations were not difficult for me.

In the dusk, straw and hay fires burned in long rows on the opposite bank, silent signals as night fell. They reminded me of the lit-up towns on the other side of the river where I had been born. Even destruction could create magical pictures, and so, with my old fondness for paradox, I thought of war as an aesthetic problem.

Change of position. We marched up to the Dnieper bridge, and then came the command to hold a strongpoint way in the east. In a mild blizzard, we crossed the Ukhlyast, a frozen swamp with few discernible paths, over man-made channels and pontoons into the unknown.

Momoshino, our goal, was like an island. The moon burned down like iced fire. Advent.

THE STRONGPOINT MOMOSHINO

We lived on an island in no-man's-land. Momoshino, a totally obscure hamlet consisting of a few huts and barns, was made into a strongpoint. There was a trench dug around the village, studded with many machine-gun nests. Infantry artillery pieces and mortars stood between the huts, and we set up our cannons just behind the trench, camouflaged as a trash heap.

We moved into a potato cellar. We unpacked, built ourselves pallets, a table and stools, installed a window and a stove, and felt we'd be here for a while. Ahead of us the land tumbled down a gully; on the other side rose a hill with tiny pines and sparse bushes. The Russians occupied their earth holes only at night. To the north, flares climbed behind the little witchy wood. There, somewhere, was the next strongpoint, between us wood, moor, and flat plain. Irregular rifle fire rang out from distant hills. A Russian storm troop was on its way. Suddenly searchlights came on opposite and combed the territory. Blindly I plunged back into the dark. The front became restless. An hour later heavy fire sounded from the north, from the direction of the Dnieper bridge.

We weren't surprised when orders came that we were moving to a new position.

After midnight we marched in bright moonlight to the road. Behind us the bunker was burning down. The fire slowly receded as we left the enemy behind. No-man's-land all around. We passed through Selez. It had become a ghost village just behind the main fighting line, pocked by trenches and bunkers and crisscrossed by the veins and intestines of war. Close to the Dnieper, we set up our gun on a hill at the edge of a pinewood. In front of us a stream flowed through swampy, half-frozen pastureland. The wood was already in enemy hands. It didn't seem possible to escape; the river was too close.

Exhausted, we wrapped ourselves in our blankets, lay down in the shelter of young pines on the soft pine-needle-sown ground, and slept. Next day we built a dugout, spread birch boughs over it, covered it with tarpaulins and hay, brought in straw to rest on, and set up the stove we took with us everywhere. We weren't able to sit in it, and the stove didn't generate much heat. But we had a roof, at least, we were sheltered from snow and wind, and we slept well.

We woke up with rheumatic pain, alarmed by shots, shouts, and cries for help. Our rear guard appeared at the edge of the wood, fled across the swamp, pursued by the Russians, until they found shelter next to us among the trees. We lobbed out some shells. Laid down a machine-gun barrage. For all their superior numbers, the enemy withdrew.

In the gray, icy winter, we lived in the open air. In the pinewood, we were out of sight of the Russians, a bit of frozen snow still lay in the hollows, and we easily bore the cold. No one bothered with us, only the field kitchen visited us at night, and so we were the only free men around at the time. Toughened and lazy, we let life do with us what it would.

[*Note:* Gap in the manuscript]

where the enemy's scout parties would rendezvous at night. The field kitchens would come up from the south in a sort of convoy, closely guarded, under cover of darkness, and still there were always losses, wounded, killed, and often missing. The Russians took a lot of captives, they were no longer killing them, as they had once done at Mileyevo, and we, in daily expectation of such a fate, were now less worried about it.

We were living on a sort of island, in a Red Army sea. Sometimes the Russian scout parties would stroll through the village quite unmolested; often there were little skirmishes. We were on alert day and night. The houses were vacated one by one, were hit by incendiaries or burned down, and even the new-moon nights were bright with flames and distant conflagrations.

So close to death, on the dividing line between a soldier's freedom and falling into enemy hands, I took to writing out my Russian adventures once more. Night after night. Outside, the sentry's footfall crunched on the snow; machine guns barked out; isolated shells whistled past. Russian nights, and I felt so much at home. Advent and Christmas passed. I stayed up, lived in my memories, and wrote. Some mornings I went to pick up mail and orders way in the hinterland; it was like visiting another island.

Daybreak. I wandered silently in the foggy land, and the road was broad. Somewhere other gray-clad pilgrims were traveling into infinity. Overhead the stars were twinkling out. The road seemed to go on forever; birch trees and conifer woods left ghostly intimations of themselves. All things had a wondrous form, but the landscape remained dead. Mute. Only the fog drifted. Deepest silence surrounded my tracks, as if I were somewhere in space. Behind me, I heard voices, messages from the past, indescribably remote.

But the wintry land came to life. Bushes and stars reached out their hands in friendship; snowy light and fog disappeared; morning air blew on me like God's breath. I was alone, and a melancholy singsong chimed in me. The snow barely crunched underfoot. The wind played in my hair. I almost had to force myself to remember that there was a war on and that I was a soldier. I believed in my destiny once more and in what was irreducibly human, some angelic force that was stronger than everything contrary, a sanctuary, preserving whatever was best and most characteristic in me across the gulf of the years.

Christmas passed like any other day. We drank a lot, but we didn't celebrate.

The year fell back into God's hands; a new one came trundling out of the basket of eternity. Only dreams remained: dreams of returning home and of peace. We were still living in the subterranean soldiers' town of Momoshino and compared ourselves with those monks in India immured in magical temples and forests. Existence pressed in upon us and marked us. The soul built wall after wall around itself and concealed itself from the din of history. It was like a dream; it was true in some magical sense. Like sleepwalkers, we passed over the mystical bridge of life. But all around us we heard the grandeur and the decline of the West, adventurers' blood pounded in our veins, our curiosity about foreign parts was satisfied in abundance, and only homesickness remained true to us in the end.

We moved out once more. The Russians had broken through. We could hear the sounds of a battle to the rear of us. We marched.

We wandered through the smoke and flames of Momoshino. Fires were reflected in the snow. The night gleamed bloodred. We stopped at daybreak, and in the evening we moved into position in a wood near Malo-Krassnitza. I became a runner and had more sleep and more time.

A light conifer wood. We were near its edge, under continual fire from machine guns and shells. The Russians didn't attack, and one of our storm troops got no farther than no-man's-land. The winter grew severe. Hoarfrost ornamented the trees, like the soul of the twigs, suddenly made visible. I loved the wood; the snow on fir and pine in golden sun, hoarfrost on full-moon nights, and a baffling disquiet often sent me out at night. I loved life, winter, and danger. It was as though I were now bringing in the harvest of a long and productive time.

I had become an adventurer, a wandering mendicant, a vagabond. The war sent me hither and thither like chaff; there seemed no end to my wanderings. But I loved life, winter, and peril. Whatever I lost was really gain. What I saw in loneliness and grief acquired a magical meaning. Whatever I had failed to do was completed, only bigger, and whatever I beheld struck me as being my own work. I stood there calmly, the earth fell into my open hands, and God was near to me. Time and eternity rushed past me. I loved life.

Sleigh rides. I flew through the forest. The wind blew and soughed in the branches, the horses panted, and the night became a dreamy, drunken revel. Frightened travelers jumped aside; a dusting of snow flew up. The runners creaked and crunched. A bold song was on my lips. Like clouds and stars, I chased through the sleeping land, plain, solitude, ravished by youth and speed. There was no end in sight. Yearning plunged into the distance; frost caught in my hair. Rushing passage, as on a sleigh in space. An intoxicating feeling came over me: a burgeoning sense of life, the limitless, exuberant pleasure of being in the world. The freedom of an hour in the Russian winterland. I loved life.

Years charged by, death wheeled over the earth, God and his stars perished in the West, and there was war on earth. I was a soldier in danger and in pain, a wanderer, a traveler in space. But I loved life.

PAUSE

Pause. A furlough, a leave. Home! Home! But it was just an interval. The war went on. Once more I went out there.

I loved life.

Notes

xxiv Many common soldiers: Wette, Wolfram, *Die Wehrmacht: Feindbilder, Vernichtungskrieg, Legenden*, S. Fischer, Frankfurt-am-Main, 2002.

4   I was working: Reese was a trainee with the Duisburger Bankverein.

6   on Darss: Reese is referring to the Fischland-Darss-Zingst peninsula on the Baltic Sea.

7   On my twenty-first birthday: Reese confuses his twenty-first birthday with his twentieth, on January 22, 1941. His error is presumably attributable to the chaotic circumstances attending the writing. However, Reese's cousin Hannelore thinks he may have deviated deliberately from conventional dating and used the date of his birth as his first birthday to make himself a year older.

12 Villages and hills: Reese is drafted to Cologne-Mülheim on February 7, 1941. He encounters the bullying of his trainers "smugly as a fat infant," because he is still convinced that everything military will come off him like water off a duck's back. He goes out to the exercise ground at Elsenborn in the Eifel only on June 29, 1941, after the completion of basic training. There he sees, to his astonishment, that there are aspects of a soldier's life that he enjoys. He is overcome by "a rare feeling of happiness" that he finds bewildering.

18 And the Wehrmacht reports: Germany attacked the Soviet Union on June 22, 1941—in other words, during Reese's military training in Cologne and the Eifel. In the first few months of the campaign, the Wehrmacht achieved great successes that made a speedy victory, as previously against France, appear possible.

20 Reese boards his train east in Cologne at the end of August. On the eve of his departure, he notes he is glad the period of uncertainty is now over. In his first days in Poland he hopes not to have to fight, since the war against the USSR will presumably be over before he can get to the front.

22 In the morning: Reese is stationed in this small town (which today is in southern Poland) from August 24 to September 24, 1941. Following the German attack on Poland, Soviet troops occupied the east of that country. Jaroslaw was close to the new demarcation line.

30 We got off: This town fifty kilometers southwest of Kiev was taken by the Wehrmacht on September 19, 1941. Reese enters it a few days later.

31 But even if we didn't believe: Peasants.

32 We rode to Kiev: The day before Reese reaches the German-held city of Kiev, September 28, 1941, one of the greatest encirclements of the war is concluded east of the city, with 650,000 Soviet soldiers taken prisoner. In letters shortly afterward, Reese writes about seeing a line of 10,000 prisoners. As Reese leaves Kiev for the east, the genocide of Ukrainian Jews is already under way behind the front. In the ravine of Babi Yar, more than 30,000 Kiev Jews are shot.

34 They in turn starved: When Reese arrives in Glukhov on October 14, 1941, the German advance is already being slowed down by a combination of mud, early snow, and the exhaustion of the troops. By the middle of October the order from the high command to Army Group Center to prosecute the attack on Moscow, Operation Typhoon, can no longer be followed.

37 We showed off: In spring 1944 Reese composes some handwritten "supplements" to this passage. The following was found in his papers, undated:

No one knew where the front was. We marched into the unknown and were distributed among various battalions. We tramped through ankle-deep, knee-deep mire, & in the evening, darkness fell with rain and fog. I stayed behind with the last of the vehicles, clung on to the cart, and allowed myself to be dragged along. A village, the outlines of the houses, dim lights on in some windows! The driver gave the horses their head and fell asleep; I had my eyes closed till a stumble brought me around; the cart had skidded into a ditch and toppled over. Ammo, blankets, and gear were lying in the mud; the horses were too enfeebled to get up, entangled in reins and harness, wallowing and kicking under the axle! — The driver went to get help, I sat down on the blankets to wait. It started to rain, and I took refuge in a house. I walked in like a ghost, claggy, pale, with dead eyes; the woman brought me milk, the little girl offered me her bowl of porridge, and I ate. I shared my chocolate with her. Then I felt I couldn't hold back my tears and went outside, it was a terrible thing to be human and a soldier. — My comrades returned. We pushed the cart up onto the roadway, harnessed the horses again, and marched on into the darkness. I plunged into a drainage ditch. The cold crawled up me; I hurried on. Once arrived, I hid under a bed, lay on thin straw among rags and cats, shivering too much to sleep. At least no one found me, so I didn't have to go on watch, & so the night passed.

Once again we were marching under the same gray skies, through rain & muck in hilly country. The villages went by without our learning their names. We overnighted in a school on a hill, put the guns under cover any old how, but the exhaustion made us too dull to protect ourselves. We didn't know if we were a long way behind our lines, or in no-man's-land, or just behind the fleeing Russians. We weren't interested in fighting, we were just marching, and in misery.

Fatesh. We had a house; we were roasting geese and eating rye farm bread. Then we had to go on sentry duty, almost an hour through the dull night to a collective farm, where our guns were parked. Each man stayed up for an hour, while a couple of us slept in the cellar among rats and shit, on cold stones, so exhausted we could barely rally ourselves when it was time to go back. —

Destiny tormented us, but we hated ourselves. Charity died in us; where nothing bonded us, there was no door open for God either. I read the New Testament, but I couldn't say why; I tried to hold on to the words — they were my last shield against emptiness — but they remained inert. No teaching that hadn't been lived could master this life. The time felt constricted, the spirit shriveled, & finally everything was just a yell of despair. We had to hate each other; whoever thought about love was doomed to break against the carapace of his own fate.

God and the stars were rooted in suffering; the soldiers' anguish gave birth to angels, demons, gods, and genii, & war produced the spirit of the future. Only we couldn't discern any limits, so there was no completion. — It was then I first encountered death; it didn't threaten me, but I saw its naked reality. I saw the first casualties of the war; they were Russian soldiers who had attacked a village, breaking out of an encirclement, murdered the unsuspecting men, looted, and were driven off by our advance guard. — They were lying in ditches and stubble fields, mute brown shapes, clenched fists, as the shells left them, and beside their shoulders grass sprouted and autumn flowers bloomed, & the rain washed the blood off their coats and hands. — I stood a long time beside one man, with whom I had once shared a condition. I thought nothing, said nothing. The dead man was more eloquent than I. He said: All up, destroyed life, war, and the indignity of death. He lay there unburied, behind him a row of birch crosses, over people whom he might have shot. Now nothing could tell them apart. — There were no angels conversing at the head of this corpse, no spirits were mourning him, & nothing graced his resting place except grass and corn, the stars at night, washed by rain; crows pecked into him. That was death. — It wasn't till then that I understood that I could one day die myself, that death and danger were not notions. But I didn't really grasp the truth of it. It didn't hurt; just the misery of daily life felt a little worse. We marched on.

Life had been put on like a mask, so that its sufferings might atone for some unknown thing. No one could see his own guilt, but it had to be immense. Didn't one day like this make up for a thousand crimes?

I wore the mask of a warrior; another two years, and I started to act the part, but I never really became *it. I couldn't do it and didn't want to do it — not until I died myself, height of futility, would I* be *it.*

38 Kursk: Reese reaches Kursk at the beginning of November 1941. On November 6, before the Supreme Soviet, Stalin reckoned Soviet casualties as 350,000 dead, 378,000 wounded, and more than a million missing. In the middle of November, the second phase of Operation Typhoon started, with the exhausted and poorly equipped German troops advancing to within a few dozen miles of Moscow.

39 We set out: The attack on the town thirty miles northeast of Kursk begins in the final weeks of November; it is taken on December 4, 1941.

44 He began with: A popular folk song celebrating the memory of Stepan "Stenka" Timofeyevich Razin, the leader of a peasants' uprising in southern Russia in the seventeenth century.

45 Then we marched: The little river flows north between Kursk and Voronezh. At the end of November 1941 the mercury falls to thirteen below (Fahrenheit). The Wehrmacht is forced to admit that the Soviet Union will not fall in the course of that year.

46 We never learned: On December 5 and 6, 1941, the Soviet winter offensive begins with fresh troops. The small town of Nikolskoye (which is perhaps what is meant by "Nikolausdorf"), where Reese sees action between Arinok and Volovo, is on the eastern bank of the Tim. In mid-December, Hitler prohibits any further withdrawal and calls for "fanatical resistance."

50 The outpost was: Here Reese is fighting some ninety miles northeast of Kursk, from December 12 to December 25, 1941. Soviet troops made an advance immediately before his arrival. By year's end 174,000 German soldiers have been killed on the eastern front, 36,000 are missing, and 604,000 wounded.

54 We left our cannons behind: The fight for and flight from the small town of Urynok on the Tim, some twenty-five miles south of Livny, took place on January 18 and 19, 1942. "We left everything when we fled, I hung on to maybe 150 cigarettes. Now I am very poor," Reese writes in his diary. Many months later he still refers in letters to "the tragedy of Arinok" as one of the crucial experiences of the war for him.

59 In Ostroleka Mazowieckie: On March 13, 1942, Reese writes his parents he was now at the "Reserve Military Hospital Ostrov.-Maz (Warsaw District), Block 1c, Ward 18." Evidently this refers to Ostroleka Mazowieckie, about forty miles northeast of Warsaw. Throughout the train journey taking many days, Reese is afraid of being turned back into the danger zone. "The last hurdle, so help me God," he writes in his calendar.

62 When I got home: Reese reaches the hospital in Offenbach at the end of March 1942. From the beginning of May he is in barracks in Cologne. Then from May 11 till the end of June, he is on leave.

63 With cheerful intuitions: The second tour to the eastern front begins on June 21, 1942. As late as his presentation for inspection a few days before, Reese is unsure whether he will be sent to Russia or France.

70 Stations and buildings: As the fourth largest city in the Soviet Union and a major nodal point, Kharkov was the subject of intense fighting. Four weeks before Reese's arrival, there was the encirclement southeast of Kharkov. The site of genocide Drobitzki Yar is close by; once the remaining Jews of Kharkov had been starved, used as hostages, tortured, and locked up, a special commando set about their systematic extermination, beginning in January 1942.

71 We dubbed ourselves: The excursion of the Rosenkavaliers took place on July 3, 1942. The German summer offensive began not many days previously.

73 Warsaw: Reese reaches the hospital in Warsaw on July 13 or 14, 1942.

79 And so we came: Reese offers no detailed account of the stops between his time in the hospital in Warsaw and his next departure for Russia. Following two weeks in Warsaw, he is returned to Germany, where he receives treatment in Neubrandenburg and is sent to barracks in Cologne at the end of August. He starts learning Italian. On August 25, 1942, he writes, "end of hospital," and the following day, "celebrate return with Mama and Papa." In the middle of October 1942 he travels via Warsaw and the Baltic to the Rshev area, which he reaches on October 23, 1942. Rshev is in the Kalinin district, 120 miles northwest of Moscow.

85 My comrades were dispatched: Appears as Olenino on army maps.

85 So, in the middle: The account here appertains to November 1942. "I'm lying here, to look after the things," he writes to his parents at the end of the month.

95 We experienced the beginning: Reese writes to his parents about this New Year's Eve in the following terms: "So much noise was not a small matter, given that what our division uses up in terms of munitions in a quarter of an hour comes to about 100,000 marks."

101 That was salvation: Reese is wounded on February 9, 1943. In relief he writes home: "There's only about an inch between the entry and exit wounds, and it's in the soft tissue on the inside of the thigh. It

happened at half past eleven, as I crept out of the bunker to clean out the chimney, and was so incautious as to stand upright, because I was dazzled by the sun (I had inflamed eyes, but they're better now). A Russian marksman made the most of the opportunity, for which I must thank him."

103 The next evening: The Lithuanian town is called Virbalis today and is close to the border of what was then East Prussia.

104 I traveled via Dresden: Reese arrives in Thuringia on February 19, 1943. The photograph used on the front cover of the present book was taken then, in Oberhof. Reese comments on March 31: "Oberhof's doughty street photographer took my picture on Saturday, with the enclosed results. I prefer myself without cap, but it's all right. One shouldn't demand too much of oneself."

106 Life went on: From mid-May 1943, Reese is in Friedrichshafen. He leaves in early June for the barracks in Cologne-Wahn. There he witnesses the bombing raids on the city. He visits the cinema, the concert hall, the church. He tries in vain to find some sustenance in faith. Following mass in Bonn Cathedral, he writes: "I wish I could see the point in it—but I can't. The organ playing is much more divine than the wine the priest drinks." Following a trip to the Drachenfels in the Siebengebirge, he rides back down on a donkey. In his diary he mentions talking to it: "Today you carry me, tomorrow it's my turn to carry you." On July 12 he boards a train for the eastern front again.

110 This was my house: In his letters he refers to this house, which he also draws, as the villa. He lives there till August 13, 1943, when his unit withdraws from the advancing Soviet forces. He is in the environs of the Vopez River, which flows into the Dnieper near Yarzevo, from mid-July on.

115 Our troops advanced: Reese arrives on July 24, 1943. The battle is in progress from the day after until August 1. Even before the fighting begins, he is prey to violently fluctuating feelings; on July 21 he writes "Help me, God!" in his diary. After the ride on the horse-drawn baggage cart, he records that his mood was "even lower." Army maps show a place by the name of Mileyevo, roughly five miles northeast of Kvastovitchi. Not far from there is another town by the name of Panov.

119 It wasn't the nearness: The detailed account of this battle in Reese's diary shows how closely the book follows his notes and records, as well as how much he has worked on his account. Diary and manuscript tally down to minor matters of detail. For instance, the entry for July 26, 1943, shows:

Flies. Began letter to parents, etc. but no courage to send it. I first want to know more about what will happen to me here. I write behind the artillery piece in a foxhole. Seven a.m. Cool, windy, overcast, I'm cold. The attack began yesterday at 1715, while the 3rd battalion already embattled in the morning and took many losses, while making some progress. Whereas now the 1st battalion is in the center, ourselves and the bicycle squadron, two machine guns and 3 bazookas are there to secure the flank and drive forward. We left the village then by platoon through a swamp, from which my feet are still wet. In position halfway up the back of the hill. From the flares we could see the 1st B. being pushed back; then the Russians started coming out of the woods 600 yards in front of us. We dragged the gun back through the swamp, fired off 3 rounds, in spite of orders, ineffectual, aided by infantry. On the heights, we came under intense fire—more accurate and deadly than in the cornfield where we'd lain before, smoking. Ernst Wolf fell a step in front of me; Jupp Kramer was wounded next to me; two infantrymen ahead of us were badly wounded; another cannon also had casualties, one dead, several wounded. We almost collapsed as we pulled, and the sweat is still drying. At last the horses and limbers came to our aid; we limbered up and chased back at a gallop, I was grabbing on to the limber hook, lost my helmet and rifle. I have a replacement rifle and my cap camouflaged with corn, mosquito net down my neck. The Russians took up positions at the edge of the forest. We stayed up all night in the streaming rain that leaked through the canvas; one cannon lost, smoking greedily under canvas. Quiet night. We heard: 3rd Company had 15 dead, 14 wounded, and various missing, fate unknown; 2nd Company is scattered, 3 men come back late at night, 1st Battalion down to 22 men. Myself exhausted and shy, helpless, shattered from seeing so much death. The bodies still lying there, badly wounded only picked up toward morning, 25 belly wounds still untreated in the aid station, many more must have died there. I'm shivering, my eyes are falling shut. But cold, shaking, and fire from heavy Russian weapons keeping me awake. Several times, hails of shrapnels rained down. Wish I could sleep. Sleep for a long, long time—and then wake up at home. Dream as I drop off: a black-and-gray-striped newt in a puddle. 1600 hrs. At 0500 the Rus-

sians attacked; we saw them emerging from the forest in long lines, while machine guns and shells kept us covered. I loaded, and Willi Dahlhoff shot; artillery and bazooka fire stopped the attack in front of us. To the right of us, the Russians broke into the village, no communication with the left. Almost all the reservists wounded or dead, just 6 of us left here, I was in despair, the end seemed nigh, praying. Last thoughts of my dearest, and my parents. Suddenly news that 2nd Company and 1st Battalion on their way with battlefield weapons. I broke down and wept [. . .]

125   The retreat began: In the summer of 1943 the Wehrmacht's last great offensive on the eastern front, code-named Operation Citadel, failed. The Germans were pushed back behind their starting positions. Orel and Kharkov were given up. Henceforth the Wehrmacht is permanently on the defensive, and the destruction of towns and villages that has already begun is intensified.

141   I got myself bandaged up: Reese is wounded on September 13, 1943. In his diary he writes that while the actual wound doesn't hurt, his whole head does. "Only 1 little splinter, I was incredibly lucky, but by that same token it's not enough to get me home." A day later he notes that he has "deep, dull fear, fear of death, fear of living—it's ghastly."

143   We marched: Withdrawal to the so-called panther position behind the Desna River.

145   We had covered: Reese and his unit have now—mid-September 1943—come to the region thirty-eight miles southwest of Bryansk. The line through Pochep links the towns of Bryansk and Gomel.

149   We wrote letters: Reese tells his parents in letters of the lootings and orgies along the line: "I had a lot of red wine to drink, slept well, and at seven this morning I made myself scrambled eggs with four eggs and quite a bit of bully beef" (September 21, 1943). "The villages are looted, chickens, cows, sheep, carrots, and potatoes rounded up, and fires lit all along the length of the train, cooking and roasting and lipsmacking" (September 22, 1943). "I must have put on another five pounds already" (September 23, 1943).

149   We sang over: The town on the east bank of the Dnieper is given up by the Germans at the end of November 1943, after bitter fighting. In the years before, it became clear how the perpetrators of the Holocaust were rampaging behind the Wehrmacht's lines and occasionally in col-

laboration with it. Before the war, about a third of the inhabitants of Gomel were Jews. Following the German occupation, they are made to wear stars. A ghetto and four camps are set up. In one of them Jews are interned and made to clear minefields at the front. Thousands of Jews are murdered for assisting the partisans; women and children are gassed.

153 We were saved: According to Reese's notes, the battle lasted from October 11 to 17, 1943. In the following weeks more and more of the Wehrmacht is moved behind the line of the Dnieper.

160 Momoshino: The village of Momoshino is in the swampy rising of the Ukhlyast River, a tributary of the Dnieper.

165 I loved life: Until the beginning of 1944 Reese is in various postings in the area of the Dnieper. At Christmas 1943 he is promoted to acting bombardier. The sleigh ride described at the end of the account takes place on January 12, 1944. Like much else in his war book, Reese first describes his sudden emotional outburst in a letter to his parents: "The night was a dreamy, drunken revel. Alarmed travelers leaped aside; more and more I was taken by this intoxication, this delirious feeling of life, this limitless desire to be in the world." Two days later he looks into the future full of optimism. Though he has lost much that was good and fine and his own and has been deprived of happiness, joy, and faith, there is "still enough for a cornerstone of a new life—in peace."